D0202222

More Things You Need to Be Told

A Guide to Good Taste and Proper Comportment in a Tacky, Rude World

By the Etiquette grrls

Lesley Carlin *and* **Honore McDonough Ervin**

BERKLEY BOOKS, NEW YORK

A Berkley Book
Published by The Berkley Publishing Group
A division of Penguin Group (USA) Inc.
375 Hudson Street
New York, New York 10014

PRINTING HISTORY
Berkley trade paperback edition / June 2003

Library of Congress Cataloging-in-Publication Data

Carlin, Lesley, 1973–
    More things you need to be told : a guide to good taste and proper comportment in a tacky, rude world / the Etiquette Grrls, Lesley Carlin and Honore McDonough Ervin.— Berkley trade pbk. ed.
        p. cm.
    ISBN 0-425-19018-8
    1. Etiquette for young adults. I. Ervin, Honore McDonough, 1975– II. Etiquette Grrls. III. Title.

BJ1857.Y58C365 2003
395—dc21

                                                                        2003044401

CONTENTS

CHAPTER TWO:
"Where the Boys Are": Boys and Chivalric Behavior   33

CHAPTER THREE:
"I'm Gonna Sit Right Down and Write Myself a Letter": Letters for All Occasions   54

CHAPTER FIVE:
It's Money, Baby!   130

CHAPTER SIX:
Gifts and Greediness   152

ACKNOWLEDGEMENTS

The Etiquette Grrls are most grateful to . . .

—Douglas Stewart, our Brilliant Agent, and everyone at Curtis Brown

—Hillery Borton, for Simply Everything

—Kelly Groves and Jennifer Slattery, our Incomparable Publicists

—Christine Zika and all at Penguin Putnam and Berkley

—The Dear Readers of EtiquetteGrrls.com, who never fail to Shock, Amaze, and Amuse us with Their Queries

—Peter Hopkins of Gargan Communications, and Everyone at Crane & Co. for being So Swell

—Our Dear Friends and Colleagues, who Know Who They Are

Lesley sends special thanks to her parents, Joan and John Carlin, for being the consummate EGs Cheering Section; to Stephanie, Adam, and Brett, for their keen appreciation of both Sarcasm and Gin—they are, collectively, The Bee's Knees; to the McElhattan family; to everyone at Her Day Job for putting up with EGs Business; to Oscar, Rory, and Leopard, the *Exceedingly* Well-Behaved Etiquette Pets; and, as ever and with much love, to her husband, Josh McElhattan.

Honore is especially thankful for the support of her family. She is also indebted to Mark, for being the Etiquette Guardian Angel, and Going Above and Beyond the Expected Duties of any Confirmation Sponsor. Thanks also to the entire Trumpbour Clan, for sending along all the clippings from all corners of the world, and being, in essence, a very well-staffed PR Firm. Last, but most certainly not least, she sends beaucoup de thanks to Amy, Chay, Melanie, Celina, Robert, Mark, Pip, and Dean for being so Loyal, Patient, Encouraging, and Amusing while she had her (frequent) fits of frustration whilst working on this volume; for all of the G&Ts (avec Bombay Sapphire, or better yet, Boodle's); and best of all, for Just Being There.

TYNTBT 2.0 is for all of you, with Our Thanks.

INTRODUCTION

Once upon a time, the Etiquette Grrls couldn't imagine anything worse than some Insipid Fool wearing a Tube Top in Church. The very image gave us the Vapors! It sent us running for Gin! And it made us take Pen to Paper, in the hopes that we could help Cure the World of Rudeness. Thus was born EtiquetteGrrls.com, our pink-and-green website, and *Things You Need to Be Told*, our first book. Oh, Dear Reader, how the EGs had visions of waking up the day after that book was published to find everyone gallantly relinquishing seats on the subway to the Elderly, the Weak, and the Pregnant; of Young Apartment Dwellers fixing up their flats into Presentable Places, instead of milk crate–filled dumps with sheets thumb-tacked over the windows; of all persons, regardless of situation, being Appropriately Dressed! Thank-You Notes would stuff Mailboxes to the point of bursting! Cell 'phone usage would Cease! And Lite Beer and Wine Coolers would just gather dust on the Liquor-Store Shelves!

Well, like most Visionaries, perhaps the EGs were just un peu Ahead of Ourselves avec Our Utopia. It seems that the more people we meet, the more stories of Unfathomable Rudeness we hear. Cell 'phones are ringing during Funeral Masses—and, worse, people are answering them! Thousands of Wedding Invitations are being mailed avec Registry Information inside—and people are demanding "Cash in lieu of Gifts"! Otherwise well-behaved, polite people turn into Raving, Rude Lunatics behind the wheels of their cars! Sixty percent of the U.S. Population *still* cannot seem to Grasp the Concept that One Does Not Wear White Shoes After Labor Day or Before Memorial Day, no matter how many times the Etiquette Grrls repeat it!

All of this, as you might imagine, Dear Reader, is Not Good.

Yet rather than throw up our hands and Barricade Ourselves in the Etiquette Flat, awaiting the Apocalypse with nothing but a Well-Stocked Bar, beaucoup de Olives and Artichokes, a lot of Well-Worn Evelyn Waugh Novels, and a Vintage Hi-Fi to keep us entertained, we set about trying, yet again, to Effect Some Positive Change. We realized that one book was Not Possibly Enough—there was, simply, Far Too Much More to Be Said. Our Readers wanted to throw Smashing Cocktail Parties, but what would they Converse About at them? Our Readers' Small Pets *demanded* the EGs' Sage Advice! ("How," they asked, "could they be more like the EGs' own Small, Well-Mannered, Intelligent Pets?") And although we made it Pretty Damn Clear that Thank-You Notes are Not Optional, many Dear Readers, suffering from Writer's Block, begged the EGs to pen a few samples to use as models. The result was the very cleverly titled volume you are now holding in Your Hot Little Hands—*More Things You Need to Be Told*! Or, as we have come to refer to it, *TYNTBT 2.0*. We do hope you find it helpful, Dear Reader.

Lastly, as means of Introduction, the EGs would like to get a couple of Particularly Annoying Questions out of the way: First, "Aren't Good Manners just for Rich, Snobby Phonies?" This, Dear Reader, is, quite frankly, the Single Most Ridiculous Thing We Have Ever Heard! Everybody can, nay, *should,* be well-mannered, witty, gracious, and A Generally Keen Person *regardless* of their Income Tax Bracket! Second, "Isn't this, like, kind of Irrelevant? Especially in a Post–September 11th World? Who cares about etiquette *now*?" Au contraire, we say! Etiquette is based on Consideration, Respect, Common Sense, and an Appreciation for Tradition—how, Dear Reader, could that *possibly* be Irrelevant? *Especially* now! "These are the times that try men's souls," Our Dear Thomas Paine wrote, and we say it is the Times That Try Men's Souls that call for being on Your Best Behavior. The EGs firmly believe one can have a Smashing Career, a Packed Social Schedule, and All Manner of Electronic Wizardry at one's fingertips and still be Polite, Stylish, Witty, and Gracious. Does it take effort? Of course, but for Heaven's Sake, dashing off a Thank-You Note is not exactly Hard Labor! Does it take a lot of money? No, not a Single Red Cent, Dear Reader. Do you have to live in the Northeastern United States to be Polite, Stylish, Witty, and Gracious? Dear Reader, don't be Ridic! From Sea to Shining Sea, not to mention Abroad, Polite Behavior in a Tacky, Rude World is a possibility for Everyone, Everywhere. And c'mon, you know the EGs—we're not going to go off boring you with twenty thousand ways to word complicated wedding invitations! So mix up a pitcher of G&Ts, Dear Reader, throw an Ella Fitzgerald CD in the stereo, and read on . . . there are many More Things You Need to Be Told.

More
Things You Need
to Be Told

All Yield to the Etiquette Volvo: Your Beautiful Automobile and How to Drive It Politely

Selecting an Automobile:
What You Should Be Driving

Golly, Dear Reader, there are so many Fabulous Cars out there! Now, the EGs do not claim to be Automobile Enthusiasts, but as many say about Fine Art, We Know What We Like. First, of course, if you are so lucky as to inherit or be able to afford a Really Keen Vintage Automobile, you absolutely must take advantage of it! Heck, the EGs would find ourselves Highly Motivated to learn to drive a Stick-Shift if a Darling Old MG were Thrust Upon Us! The EGs adore Nice Old Automobiles, from Vintage T-Birds to Mercedes Roadsters . . . when Kept Up, or Splendidly Restored, they really are the Ne Plus Ultra of Cars.

Sadly, though, few of us actually have a Vintage Automobile. (And no, Dear Reader, your Mid-1980s Chevy Celebrity doesn't count as Vintage.) Where then to turn? The Etiquette Grrls remind you that your car should be both Useful and Safe, no matter its cost. This means that if you live in a Sedate, Coastal New England Town, and Your Driving consists of Running Out to the Market, visiting the Tennis Club, and picking up your Wee Ones after Soccer Practice, you have No Business buying a Ferrari of any sort, or, really, any other Flashy Sports Car. And there is no excuse whatsoever for driving a car that has any Essential Parts either missing or affixed to the car avec Duct Tape.

Do the EGs like some Expensive Cars? Yes. But we like Expensive Cars that don't scream, *"I AM AN EXPENSIVE DAMN CAR!"* Volvos are a good example of this. New Volvos are every bit as Luxurious as, say, BMWs, but not quite so Ostentatious. If you can't swing a New Volvo, by all means, get an Old One! Old Volvos are Fly! The EGs particularly like the Really Boxy 240 Models, which will always hold a Special Place in Our Hearts. Oh, Dear Reader, the EGs will take a 1986 Volvo 240 Wagon over a Brand-New Honda Civic any day!

What You Should Not Be Driving

The Average Person needs a plain, simple car. In other words, SUVs can See Us In Hell! The EGs doubt that most SUVs are ever used for any purpose resembling either Sport or Utility. Unless you *habitually* drive on Dirt Roads, or Haul Heavy Stuff Around, you don't need a Hulking, Gas-Guzzling, Tank-like Vehicle. Those who fancy driving Jeeps should consider Joining the Army.

What Color Car?

If you're in a Vintage Automobile, chances are you can get away with a Paint Job in Much Prettier Colors than you'll find in Modern-Day Voitures. The EGs love those Big Fifties Cars that came in light turquoise blue, cream, beautiful cherry red, and even pink! But put that same pink on Your Jetta, and you'll look Pretty Darn Silly, Dear Reader. We think that unless you have a car Worthy of a Splashy Color (such as one of the aforementioned Vintage Automobiles), it's always best to Keep It Simple. Black, grey, navy, silver, and British Racing–car Green are quite tasteful. Steer clear (tee hee!) of Anything Neon; any color Named After a Fruit (your car is not An iMac); metallic red (always vile); and gold. White is also Quite Iffy, if for no other reason, than the minute you go anywhere, Your Car will look Filthy. Also, remember that the Color of Your Car should Make You Look Good. If you're a Brunette, you could look Smashing in a dark shade of red, but if you're a Redhead, opt for dark green.

Automobile Accoutrements

Newsflash, Dear Reader: Your Car is not Your Bedroom. Nor is it Your Office, Your Closet, Your Locker, Your Library, or Your Trashcan! Therefore, keep Extraneous Matter out of Your Voiture! The Etiquette Grrls have never understood why some people cart Mittens, Scarves, Sweaters, Paperwork, Pillows, Dumbbells, Basketballs, Golf Clubs, Skis, Bicycles, Toys, Library Books, Empty Soda Bottles, and Gum Wrappers everywhere they go! Dear Reader, we highly doubt you are going to have a sudden need to do Triceps Extensions while you are In Traffic—there are better places to put such items. Similarly, while we certainly understand the importance of Having a Pair of Nice Warm Gloves around for when you must shovel your car out of a ten-foot Snowdrift, we do not appreciate having to move Said Gloves out of our way when you are driving us to the shore in July.

"Decorating" One's Car

The Etiquette Grrls just *know* that somewhere, someone is driving a new Volkswagen Beetle (in that yucky lime-green color) with a Bouquet of Fake Daisies in its silly flower holder, umpteen Pine-Tree Air Fresheners hanging from the Rearview Mirror along with some sort of New-Agey Crystal Pendant Doodad, a Fuzzy Hot-Pink

Leopard-Print Steering Wheel Cover, Beaded Seat Covers, a Phalanx of Bobble-Head Scotties, glittery bumper stickers reading "Princess" and "Rock Star," and a blue, flashing, neon license-plate holder. This madness must stop! Do not put anything in your car that is not Standard Equipment or, at least, Highly Serviceable and Plain-Looking! We don't mind your affixing a CD holder to your window shade, but we beg of you, let it not be Glittery, or Feathery, or Otherwise Ostentatious! The EGs also would like to ban what we believe are referred to as "Hot-Rod" Accessories. It is not acceptable—indeed, it is laughable—to remove the Perfectly Good Spoiler from the back of your car and replace it with a three-foot-tall one that looks like a Jet Tail. It is *particularly* ridiculous to affix accessories like spoilers and giant wheels to a car that obviously was not designed to accommodate them, such as a Toyota Minivan.

The EGs, of course, understand how much fun it is to Collect Things. We cannot stroll past the tiniest of Antique Shops sans inquiring as to their stock of Vintage Barware and if they have any Interesting Pieces in Our Silver and China Patterns! However, much as we love these things, we do not put them on display in the Etiquette Volvo. We see far too many cars with Stacked-Up Baseball Caps or Piles of Beanie Babies in the back window—how on earth can the driver *see*? Furthermore, speaking of In-Car Collections, the fact that Your Car Smells Less Than Appealing is not something you should call attention to—there is no need to display every Hanging Air-Freshener Doodad you have ever purchased! Should your car acquire a Nasty Aroma, get its Carpet Shampooed—adding a Faux Piña Colada Scent to the mix is not going to help.

Bumper stickers are one of the EGs' Pet Peeves. We wouldn't mind reading the odd interesting quote from, say, T. S. Eliot, on the bumper of the car in front of us as we are stuck in traffic, but, unhappily, this is never the case. What we *do* end up reading seems to be limited to the following stickers:

- Stupid "Euroval" stickers. If the EGs see One More Car with "ACK" or "HH" or "CC" or "MV," we are going to scream! So you've been to an Upper-Middle-Class Vacation Destination. Whoo-hoo. Get Over It. It's one thing if you and Your Car have actually Been to Europe, and Had to take a Ferry Someplace (the point of those stickers), such as from "GB" to "FR," but it's Just Ridiculous for anyplace in the United States to mimic the Serviceable European Stickers. And do we even need to tell you what we think about Schools which adopt this sticker format in lieu of the traditional clear back-window decal?

- "My Child Was Student of the Month at Blah-Blah Elementary School." We're happy your child has earned this Distinctive Honor, but is your bumper the place to announce it? What's next, "My Child Was Phi Beta Kappa, and I Bet Yours Flunked Out"? "My Child Works Ninety Hours a Week as a Management Consultant and Earns a Pile of Money"? The EGs don't much like Braggarts.

- "I ♥ My Pomeranian/Goldfish/Hairless Cat." Well, that's nice. The EGs love our Cashmere Twinsets, but we don't feel the need to Broadcast it to All and Sundry whilst we're on the road.

- "Practice Random Acts of Kindness and Senseless Acts of Beauty." Excuse us, but the EGs don't think Kindness should be Random, nor Beauty Senseless.

- "Whirled Peas." Yeah, yeah. We get it. Har, har. There's nothing like a Punny Tree-Hugger.

- "PRINCESS"/"GODDESS"/"PORN STAR"/"PIMP." We highly, *highly* doubt you are, in fact, Any of These Things (and in the case of the Latter Two, we certainly *hope* you're not).

We think it even More Bizarre that you would want to be considered to be any of them.

The EGs will make a slight exception for stickers that are Truly Different and Clever—e.g., "Ghetto Cruiser" on a Vintage MG, or " 'Creative' People Must Be Stopped" on an otherwise Mom-Like and Innocuous Station Wagon—but unless you have Perfect Pitch vis-à-vis Ironic Wittiness, you'd better play it safe and leave your bumper Stark Naked.

Also, Your Car is probably not the place to voice your Political or Religious Opinions. This is frequently offensive to others or irrelevant to them. Furthermore, whatever you do, do not leave Bumper Stickers from Old Elections on your car. You will be instantly perceived as A Gloater (if you sport the Winning Candidate) or a Whiner (if you sport the Loser). Especially if your Political Sticker is Rather Dated (e.g., "Vote Bush/Quayle!").

Your Car's Paint should be left well enough alone, Dear Reader (except for repairs in the wake of a Teeny Fender-Bender, of course). Otherwise, do not take it upon yourself to Embellish Your Paint Job. The Etiquette Grrls are quite puzzled by "Racing Stripes." Is a small line of a different color really going to make Your Car seem faster? And no, you do not need Giant, Hideous Decals *anywhere* on the Exterior of Your Car. Are you about to perform "Greased Lightning" from *Grease* in the middle of The Highway, Dear Reader? We hope not! (For a multitude of reasons!) Well, then, no Hot-Rod-Like Flames should be painted upon Your Car. We are Most Perplexed by those Redundant Stickers that point out that a certain car is, in fact, a Mazda. This is not something to be Proud Of, Dear Reader. The EGs may not be Automobile Aficionados, but really, we're not going to mistake it for a Jaguar if you Don't Remind Us.

Finally, please, please, the Etiquette Grrls beg of you, take down all that junk hanging from Your Rearview Mirror!! We are Sick and Tired of being blinded by the Prismatic Reflection off Silly

Crystal Thingies, and we do not care to see Other People's Underwear or Garters. CDs are best used in your CD player, not as Decoration.

Should I Personalize My License Plate?

In a word, *NO*. Especially if you plan to put a Cutesy-Pie Nickname on it (e.g., "SNOOKUMS"), or declare your allegiance to Your Alma Mater or Favorite Sports Team (e.g., "GOEAGLES"), or tell everyone How Old and/or Attractive You Are (e.g., "SEXY35"), or Brag About Your Academic Degree(s) (e.g., "MDPHDJD").

General Principles of Driving

There are only two real Rules of Driving Etiquette: Be Smart and Be Courteous. All of the Stupid and Rude People should be confined to their homes! Now, the EGs have no desire to play Driving Instructors, so we're not going to lecture you on How to Execute a Three-Point Turn or quiz you on Hand Signals. We would much rather outline a few things other drivers do that Drive Us Mad.

- **Driving Like a Bat Out of Hell.** The speed limit is there for A Reason. Yes, if you grew up in the Wilds of Montana, it must indeed be A Big Letdown to have to hold to sixty-five on the Pennsylvania Turnpike, but Get Over It, Leadfoot. While the EGs would never condone Reckless Driving, we do think there is a Big Difference between Driving Skillfully, Yet Fast, and Plain Old Speeding. If you honestly could Hold Your Own Safely on the Autobahn, we'll cut you a bit of slack. If not, however—especially if you're one of Those Jerks Who Swerves a Lot, Cuts People Off at ninety miles per hour and Intentionally Scares Others—we hope there's a Speed Trap out there with Your Name On It.

- **Crawling Along Like a Snail, Especially in the Fast Lane.** If there's no Horrible Traffic, or Horrible Weather, you should

be driving right around the Speed Limit. If Your Stamina or
the Decrepitude of Your Car does not permit this, Move the
Hell Over to the right, or stick to smaller roads.

- **Plain Old Cluelessness.** Leaving the Blinker On for Miles;
Driving with Your Brights On; Driving After Dark with *No*
Lights On; Getting in the Exact-Change Line at the toll booths
when you're fresh from the ATM and have only twenties . . .
this is all Highly Vexing. Pay Attention, Dear Reader!

- **Drifting Around on the Road.** Pick a Damn Lane and *stay* in
it! When you're turning, turn cleanly—don't come close to
Side-Swiping the poor folks stopped at the light when you're
making a left.

- **Thinking Your Turn Signal Is Optional,** particularly on a
Busy, Multi-Lane Street. Other Drivers are not Omniscient,
Dear Reader, and they will not expect you to make a left turn
just because you *always* turn left from State Street onto Maple
Street when you're heading to the Cinema.

- **Not Letting People Merge.** For the Love of All Things Holy,
what exactly are you hoping to gain by Being a Jerk about
this? It's not that other driver's *fault* that there's a Broken-
Down Truck in her lane and she needs to move over into
yours. Trust us, you really won't be Terribly Delayed if you
let one measly car go in front of you.

- **Stopping for No Good Reason** in places where Stopping Is
Not Expected, e.g., in Fast-Moving Traffic on the Garden State
Parkway.

- **Not Knowing Where You're Going.** See the signs indicating
"Left Lane Must Turn Left"? Well, guess what—if you're in
the Left Lane, you really *must* Turn Left! Even if you would
Rather Go Straight! You are not allowed to try to Inch Your
Way into the Center Lane, refusing to turn whilst all the Cars

Behind You (who *want* to Turn Left, and are Correctly Positioned to do so) have to wait. We all make mistakes, but this is, in fact, Your Fault, and you simply will need to find somewhere to Turn Around. Also, Dear Reader, we've all Gotten Lost, but if you need to Consult a Map, you need to Pull Over. It's not fair to hold everyone else up while you try to figure out how the heck you ended up in Lovely Downtown Bridgeport. Similarly, if you would like to ask a stranger for directions, pull over and stop. Do not make motions to "roll down the window," or Wave Frenetically at someone in the car next to yours. This looks Frightening, particularly if it's dark and you are trying to inquire of a Girl Driving Alone. The EGs are all for Helping the Lost, but if we're alone, we're sorry: Our windows will be Staying Up. Find a Gas Station and buy a map. Or better yet, keep an Atlas in Your Car in the first place.

- **Unjustifiable Use of The Horn.** Beep! BeepBeepBeep! *BEEEEEEEEEEEP!* That is *not* going to make the five-mile-long Traffic Jam move any faster, Dear Reader. It's fine to use the horn to warn another driver of Something They Don't See (e.g., they're backing out of a driveway and you're coming down the street), or to alert them to the fact that They Just Did Something Dangerous (e.g., "Hey! You're not allowed to make a Left Turn on Red and Nearly Hit Me, You Numbskull!"). It is not, however, there to help you Express Your General Frustration with Life. Wait till you get home, then compose a Cathartic Haiku or something. ("The line of traffic / stretches sans end. How I need / Gin and Cigarettes!")

- **Playing Music So Loudly People in Other Cars Can Hear It.** Dear Reader, others may not share your Deep, Abiding Love for Bell Biv Devoe/The Mormon Tabernacle Choir/ Classical Guitar/Insane Clown Posse/Enya. Even if you think Other People *should* be listening to, say, Frank Sinatra, it's not

Your Place to play his music so loudly they cannot help but hear it while they're Minding Their Own Business in the Privacy of Their Own Cars. With their windows Rolled Up.

- **Insisting One Can Drive When One Has Tossed Back Quite a Few** (and, worse, *Actually* Driving Whilst Three Sheets to the Wind). Have you been Living Under a Rock? Get a Designated Driver. Take a Taxi. Walk. This ventures beyond What's Rude into What's Illegal, and the Etiquette Grrls hope that none of our Dear Readers would even *consider* Driving Drunk! The Very Thought gives us The Vapors!

Parking

One must, of course, Get Out of One's Car occasionally, which necessitates Parking It. However, there is just Not Enough Parking in This World, and people have become Extremely Rude about it! The EGs hope Our Sage Counsel will ameliorate things.

AT HOME

When you are Searching For a New Apartment, pay careful attention to Where You Will Park Your Car. Ideally, you will have an Assigned Space, and if you're Really Lucky, this will be In a Garage, or at least Under Some Sort of Carport. (Maybe you'll even have a Valet. If this is true for you, Dear Reader, you are Très, Très Lucky, and you need to let the EGs know when there is a Vacancy in Your Building.) However, Dear Reader, at the very *least* there should be a big off-street lot with Ample Parking for All Tenants and a few spots for Guests. The EGs cannot stand City On-Street Parking and the Madness It Engenders. First of all, On-Street Parking is a Pain. There will *never* be a spot in front of Your Apartment Building when (a) it is Cold, (b) it is Raining, or (c) you need to move Something Heavy, like a Bookcase, or Several Bags of Groceries, into Your Flat. Second, On-Street Parking is Always Scarce, and thus, the spaces available are Always Small. Therefore, even if

you drive the Tiniest Mini, you will need to have a Graduate Degree in Parallel Parking in order to maneuver into them. And the
EGs have neither the Time nor the Inclination to become Expert
Parallel Parkers. Finally, there are always Complicated Rules about
exactly When, Where, and For How Long you are allowed to park
on Your Street. Is it okay from 8 P.M. 'til 7 A.M. on Monday through
Friday, except on Alternate Mondays, when the Garbage Collectors
drop by at 6 A.M. or when It Snows, in which case the Citywide
Ban on Overnight Parking kicks in, and you may only park on the
Even Side of North-South Running Streets on Even-Numbered
Days, and on the Odd Side of North-South Running Streets on
Odd-Numbered Days? What happens if you live on a Street That
Curves? How the hell are you supposed to figure out What Direc-
tion Your Street Runs, anyway? Sorry, but the EGs haven't room
for a Compass or a GPS Device in our Vintage Handbags. Arrgh!
Therefore, if Your Dream Apartment has No Parking Whatsoever,
we recommend that you either sell your car and Resign Yourself
to using Public Transportation, or look for Another Place.

ON THE STREET

Well, either you are simply Parking on the Street while you are
Visiting a Friend, or stopping at the Pâtisserie, etc., or perhaps you
just Didn't Listen to the EGs in the paragraph above and have to
leave Your Voiture on the street Every Night. In any case, if you
are going to Park on the Street, you must do so Politely.

- Make an effort not to leave Your Car too close to Anyone's
  Driveway. The person Backing Out of that driveway may be
  Mrs. Elderly Neighbor, in her Aircraft Carrier-Size Oldsmo-
  bile, and she may barrel into the grille of Your Saab.

- You must park as close to the Curb as you possibly can, especially if the Street is Narrow. It is most uncool to park so

far in the center of the Street that traffic is squeezed down to One Lane.

- If it Snows, you should shovel out your car, of course, but remember: If you park on a City Street, you do not Gain Ownership of a Particular Parking Space just because you cleared snow from it. The Etiquette Grrls have seen Utter Insanity on the Streets of Big Cities, with people leaving Ironing Boards, Garbage Cans, Big Construction Horses, etc., out to "hold their place" while they're Not In It. And we have Heard Tales of people who unwittingly parked in a space someone else thought of as Their Own having their Windows Smashed, Car Keyed, etc. We regret to inform you that even if it's in front of Your House, the Street belongs to the City, and you may not Annex Portions of It. If you wish to have a Permanent Parking Space, nothing is stopping you from Moving.

- When you're getting out of Your Car, be careful! If you're on a Busy Street, don't open the door before you ascertain that An Oncoming Vehicle will not Hit It. Also, do not inconsiderately leave your Giant Door yawning open, blocking Half the Street, while you Rummage Around for the Pesky Lipstick You Dropped.

- If Space is Tight, try to leave as much room for Other Cars as possible. Pull all the way up, so that Another Small Car can park behind you.

- Don't Double-Park. Ever. If you're waiting for one of your passengers to "run in just for *one* second" to a shop, you can Jolly Well Circle the Block a Few Times.

IN PARKING LOTS

Unless you have the Appropriate Sticker or Permit, you are Not Allowed to Park in the Handicapped Space. The EGs cannot believe the Gall of Some People! And no, just in case you were wondering, you are not allowed to *declare* yourself Temporarily Disabled because you Stubbed Your Toe, or Really Don't Feel Like Walking Very Far in Your Blahniks, etc. Unless you've got a Permit, Dear Reader, park elsewhere. (And the EGs hate to even imagine anyone would Stoop to This, but We've Seen It Happen: Unless you yourself are Disabled, or one of Your Passengers is, you have no business taking up the Handicapped Space, even if the car you're driving *has* a Permit. The EGs have heard of Young Whippersnappers borrowing Grandma's Car to go to the Mall before Christmas, so they can park right near the door, courtesy of Grandma's Permit—this is An Atrocity!)

One Car=One Parking Spot. This really shouldn't be So Difficult. However, we frequently see cars Sprawled Diagonally across Two Spaces, or Giant Pickup Trucks that are so wide they take up a good foot of the parking space next to the one they're supposed to be in. The EGs wish to remind the Thickheaded Drivers of These Vehicles that if their cars are really so valuable that *no one* can Park Near Them, they belong On Blocks in a Locked Garage. And if anyone is driving a truck or SUV that is too big for a Normal Parking Space, they should park Far, Far Away, where it won't matter so much that they're using Two Spaces. After all, you're supposed to be Rugged, n'est-ce pas? So enjoy your hike in from Lot ZZ, Mr. Lumberjack.

We've all been in the situation where the Parking Lot is Très Crowded, and several cars are Circling for Spaces. If you are the driver of such a car, and you have particularly Frail or Well-Dressed Passengers, or if you are a Boy and would like to be Chivalric toward Your Female Passenger(s), you may pull up to the entrance doors, drop them off, and arrange to Meet Up With Them in a Few Minutes, after you've found a spot.

If you're waiting for someone to Back Out of A Space, put Your Turn Signal On. Other drivers should realize that you have Dibs and allow you to take the spot. However, Dear Reader, if someone should Rudely Sneak Into a Space before you, despite the fact you've been waiting, it's probably a good idea to move along Sans Confrontation. You just can't be sure when Someone's Packing Heat.

Being Polite to Your Passengers

If you follow all of the Etiquette Grrls' Advice, you will be a Most Polite Presence on the Roads. However, Dear Reader, we would like to make sure you have a clear understanding of How You Should Treat Your Passengers. Plenty of Nascent Relationships become impossible when, on the First Date, the Boy waits outside the Girl's Apartment, Honking, and then refuses to move the Pile of Greasy Old Hamburger Wrappers off the Passenger Seat when she opens Her Own Door and attempts to get in! The EGs wouldn't want that to happen to you, Dear Reader.

First, Be On Time. If you become Stuck in a Horrible, Terrible, Unpredictable Traffic Jam, it would be a good idea to have a Cell 'Phone handy so you can let Your Passenger know you will be Late.

Obtain directions to Your Destination, stop at the Gas Station, clean out the Ashtrays, etc., *before* you pick up Your Passenger.

Never, ever wait outside someone's Home or Workplace (or, really, Anywhere) and Lean on Your Horn, hoping to Coax Them to Come Out. This is Particularly True if you are on a Date. Heavens, if anyone *dared* Honk for the EGs, we wouldn't dream of Emerging From the Etiquette Flat! (Not that the EGs would *accept* a Date with a Boy who was likely to Exhibit Such Egregious Behavior, but you get the idea of Where Your Standards Should Be, Girls.)

Boys should open doors for Female Passengers (as well as for any Guests of Honor, Elderly Gentlemen, etc., they may be transporting). You are Not Being Chivalric if you merely unlock the door for the Girl, or stretch across the seat to open it while she waits on the Sidewalk. No, no, *no,* Dear Reader, that will not do at all. Instead, you should Get Out of the Car, walk around to the Passenger Side, open the door, help the Girl into the Car (by offering your hand to lean on—do not Shove Her Into Her Seat à la The Fuzz), make sure she is seated comfortably, shut the door, then walk back to Your Side, get in, shut your door, and Begin to Drive. It's Easy!

Make certain the Interior of Your Car will be conducive to Your Passengers having a Pleasant Ride. Nothing should be In Their Way, all doors and windows should Work Properly, nothing should Smell Vile, and Trash should be disposed of in advance.

If your car itself is in Dangerous Condition (e.g., it's dark and Your Headlights Ne Work Pas), then please, make other arrangements. It is Very Rude Indeed to put Others' Lives at Risk.

Being a Polite Passenger

Isn't it nice that Someone Else is driving while you gaze out the window at the Beautiful Scenery? Ah yes, Dear Reader, it is Nice Indeed. Yet if you do not follow Certain Guidelines, chances are Your Friend will not Chauffeur You Around Again anytime soon.

If it's a long trip, offer to Take a Turn Driving. Assuming you have a License, of course, and can actually operate the Controls of the Car. (For this reason, it's Awfully Convenient to understand the intricacies of a Manual Transmission—instruction is usually available courtesy of Your Father or Your Older Brother. That is, if either of them trusts you Behind the Wheel of their vehicle.)

If it's a long trip and you cannot, for any reason, Share the Driving, you should offer to pay for Tolls and Gas, help out with Navigation, etc.

If you and a friend both have Cars, and go many places together, it's appropriate for you to Take Turns Driving. After all, it's not fair for one of you to put Miles and Miles on her car while the other's Sits Idle. (And if you frequently drive to Bars, it's quite a drag for the poor soul who is always stuck being the Designated Driver.) On the other hand, it's not nice to *insist* that the two of you *always* take Your Car, because It's Nicer, or Has a Better Stereo, or Whatever. This will make Your Friend Feel Bad. It's simply much better to Alternate.

Let's say you do not have a Car, but a friend of yours frequently drives you to the Grocery Store, always picks you up at the Airport, is willing to take you to the Remote UPS Office where Your Important Package has been left for you to Pick Up In Person, etc. Dear Reader, you are Incredibly Fortunate! *Be nice to This Person!* It would be polite of you to pay for Gas and Tolls, or, if your friend will Not Hear of This, to give your friend a Small Gift every so often to show How Much You Appreciate the Trouble They Go To. And it goes without saying that you should not Impose on This Person's Kindness and treat them as Your Personal Livery Service. ("Okay, I need to stop at the Dry Cleaner and the ATM on the way to the Airport, and when you pick me up on Monday when my flight gets in, could you stop at the Kennel beforehand and pick up My Darling Kitty, Petunia? Oh, and if you don't mind, let's go through Downtown even though it's faster to Take the Highway, 'cause I heard there's a Keen New Window Display at Saks and I'd like to see it.")

If someone is picking you up, be ready On Time. And we mean *Completely* Ready. Not, "Okay, sure, let's go. I just need to Find My Shoes, Program My VCR, and De-Lint My Coat first." If you're going to be delayed due to Circumstances Beyond Your Control (such as a delayed flight), do your best to let the driver know of the delay.

Passengers are Not Allowed to Criticize the Driver. Snide Comments ("My God, is this car powered by Turtles? We'll be lucky to get there by Nightfall!"), Rude Observations ("Hey, I didn't know Stop Signs were Optional in Connecticut!"), and Unsolicited Advice ("Okay, now you can merge . . . I *said* you could *merge* . . . Geez, easy on the brakes! . . . Okay, good, now you can move over one lane . . . Better let this guy pass you . . .") are all Extremely Impolite. If the Driver asks for Your Opinion or Advice ("Suzy, could you peek out your window and let me know if I'm too far from the Curb?"), then of course you may Offer It. Also, of course, if the Driver seems Completely Oblivious to A Great Impending Danger, you should Speak Up (*"THERE'S A TRAIN COMING!!!!"*). But if the driver is just going more slowly, or faster, than you usually do, or if they're taking a Slightly Different Route than you'd have chosen, Pipe Down.

Passengers are also Not Allowed to Criticize the Driver's Car ("Interesting that you got this model—didn't you read all the Bad Press About It?"), ask if it's *ever* Been Washed, or point out things like, "Hey, do you know there's a Dent in This Door? You might want to get that repaired—it looks awful!"

And, of course, always, *always* thank whoever drove.

"But, Officer, I Didn't Mean to . . .": Interactions Avec les Gendarmes

Oh, Dear. Suddenly there are Sirens, and Flashing Lights in the Rear-View Mirror, and there's a Very Fierce-Looking State Trooper striding up to Your Car. Oops. Dear Reader, the EGs have never, of course, received a Speeding Ticket, but let us still strive to give you some Helpful Tips on how to deal with The Police.

Never, ever, *EVER* Insult Mr. Policeman. Pull out your Best Etiquette for the conversation you will have with him. You should call him "Sir," or "Officer." Do not Play Stupid ("Tee hee, what's a 'Speed-o-meter'?"), or attempt to Flirt With Him, or try to Pass Him a Twenty. Also, this would be a bad time to mention Any Sort of Alcohol, how you've talked your way out of five other tickets today because Those Cops Back in Ohio Were *So* Stupid, or to query him on why the Police are referred to as "The Fuzz" when, in general, Cops Are Not So Fuzzy. If you have anything to discuss with Mr. Policeman pertaining to why it Might Have Been Justified for you to be Doing Eighty, you should state this very politely, very succinctly, and without a Hint of Belligerence. And honestly, Dear Reader, we're only talking about something like,

"I'm sorry, Officer, but do you see My Wife there in the Back Seat? She's Having a Baby. Right Now. In the Back Seat. I'm just trying to Get to the Hospital. Ack, is that the Head?!" Mr. Policeman really isn't going to believe anything Less Than This, and it's highly disrespectful to Lie to A Police Officer. So if you haven't An Excuse, just accept the Ticket, and dispute it In Court if you must.

Activities One May Not Engage in Whilst Driving

People are Chattering Away on Handheld Cell 'Phones! Someone is Painting Her Nails! Someone else is Using a Curling Iron while Simultaneously Shuffling through CDs and Unfolding a Map! While the Etiquette Grrls know that, sadly, People Can Be Pretty Darn Stupid, we would have thought anyone with One Functional Brain Cell would Innately Know that when one is Controlling a Big, Heavy, and Dangerous Machine that is Hurtling Along at High Speed, it is Not the Time to Multitask! The EGs remind Our Dear Readers that it is Quite Wrong to engage in any of the following activities while one is driving.

Using a Handheld Cell 'Phone is at the Top of Our Banned-Activity List. There is simply no way to dial, adjust the volume, and hold the Wee Thingamajig to Your Ear while Paying Attention to the Road! There are many Good, Affordable Headset Adaptors available for nearly all models of Cell 'Phones. Get One, and Use It. Otherwise, turn off the Cell 'Phone while you're driving, or pull off the road whenever you take or place a Call.

Grooming. Does Your Car look like Your Vanity Table? We didn't think so. Then don't use it as one! No hairstyling, no makeup application, no Tweezing, no Spa Services, no trying on Five Different Pairs of Earrings and checking how they look in Your Rear-View Mirror. This is Distracting, and thus, Dangerous, and furthermore, it makes you look Quite Idiotic.

Playing "Find That AWOL CD." It is a given that while you are in the car, all Radio Stations that come in clearly will play Nothing But Bad Music. Therefore, the Etiquette Grrls understand why so many people have CD Players in Their Cars. However, we see an Awful Lot of Drivers striking Gymnastics-esque Poses while speeding down the highway as they try to reach the One CD They Really Want to Hear, which is, inevitably, somewhere under the Passenger Seat. Dear Reader, the World Will Not End if *J to Tha L.O.* is not At Your Fingertips! (In fact, the EGs hope it's Nowhere in Your Vicinity. We're just Giving an Example.) Find a few CDs you'd like to hear before you Set Off on Your Journey, and spare the rest of us your Erratic Swerving.

Literary Pursuits. The EGs love to read. We tote a book wherever we go, in case we have a few Idle Moments. However, we do *not* attempt to read whilst driving. We're sure Your Commute is boring, but, Dear Reader, if you wish to fill the time with the Words of Great Authors, we suggest you investigate Books On Tape.

Consulting Large Maps. The Average Map, Unfolded, is usually quite similar in size to the Average Windshield. Therefore, Dear Reader, it is not a Brilliant Idea to open one up while you are at the wheel, as you will not be able to See the Road. If you must consult a Map, try to open it beforehand and refold it so that the Relevant Portion is easy to see. You may steal a glance at it while you are Stopped at Traffic Lights, or if you Pull Over.

P.D.A. The EGs disapprove of P.D.A. (Public Displays of Affection) at All Times and in All Places, but for some reason, the General Public is not heeding Our Advice, and Drivers everywhere are Smooching Their Passengers when their eyes should be on the Road! We send Our Felicitations to any couple who is So In Love, but for God's Sake, Keep Your Damn Composure until you arrive at Your Apartment! Quit Putting on a Show!

Accidents

The EGs hope we do not need to Tell You This, Dear Reader, but should you happen upon An Accident, or be Unfortunate Enough to Be Involved in One, your first obligation is to Assist Anyone Who May Be Injured. If you have a Cell 'Phone, call 911 immediately. If you are one of the Parties Involved, and there is Serious Damage to anyone's automobile, we recommend that after you have done what you can to Help the Injured, you speak to nobody but the Police. This is Not the Time to Chat About the Weather, or Trade Insider Stock Tips, or, worse, to Berate the Other Driver(s). Politely trade insurance information and All That Jazz (or wait for the Police, who will help you exchange it), and then Sit Tight. It is, of course, Embarrassing or Annoying (or both) to be involved in An Accident, but that is No Reason to be Rude to Anyone Else. If you've just witnessed a Very Serious Accident, but have not been involved, you also should Stay Put until the Police have spoken to you—the best place for you if you're not Actively Assisting Someone is sitting quietly in Your Car.

One last point: If, in the course of Your Driving, you see an accident being Tended To by the Police or An Ambulance Crew, you should continue along Your Merry Way. Do not stop and stare, pull over to take some photos in hopes of selling them to That Local Paper That Likes to Feature Blood and Gore, or roll down your window and ask questions of the Emergency Workers. Unless you are, say, a Doctor who could Offer Assistance, move on.

Other Forms of Transportation

PEDESTRIAN ETIQUETTE

You must, must, *must* be a Polite Pedestrian. The Etiquette Grrls frequently wish that we had a cunning little Cattle Prod with which we could shove Rude Pedestrians out of our path. If you are on a Crowded Sidewalk, perhaps, say, in Soho, you should not abruptly stop in order to take a swig of your Dr Pepper. You should know better, Dear Reader! Pedestrians, especially in New York, do not look where they're going, for fear of Crazy Strangers engaging them in conversation, and they will undoubtedly plow into you, setting off a Terrible Chain Reaction. If the Etiquette Grrls wanted to be trampled to death, we would frequent the Annual Bridal Gown Sale at Filene's Basement in Boston.

Similarly, if you and another pedestrian are moving on the same course in opposite directions and seem likely to collide, you ought to step aside, ideally to your right. This seems to be a particular problem with the sort of people who move in packs, who often seem to feel they have every right to bear down upon a Poor, Struggling, Lone Pedestrian attempting to carry groceries home from the store. The Etiquette Grrls remind you that the sidewalk should not be mistaken for a football field—there's no tackling allowed. You may not, under any circumstances, walk directly into another Pedestrian, push her out of your way, or body-slam her into a lamppost. Furthermore, you should take particular care not to push her into the path of an Oncoming Vehicle.

The Etiquette Grrls notice lots of pedestrians with Headphones these days. While we don't object to the practice of listening to music during the Long Trek to work or school (indeed, the Etiquette Grrls often listen to their Walkmans in an attempt—sadly, often futile—to discourage strangers from striking up a conversation with us), we do ask that you not have the volume turned up so high that you subject others to your Musical Tastes (or lack thereof). You also should not sing along with your Walkman. Save it for Your Shower.

It is quite rude to treat public spaces, e.g., sidewalks, theatre lobbies, the narthex of a commuter train, etc., as Your Personal Wastebasket. You should not toss your ABC gum where someone else might tread upon it in her fetching new ankle boots (see "When May I Chew Gum?" pages 180–181, for further information). Nor should you, say, change your Band-Aids in front of the

Kit-Kat Club and toss what is probably legally defined as Medical
Waste into a public thoroughfare.

You must not spit upon the sidewalk or, indeed, upon anything.
Ever.

What, the Etiquette Grrls ask, is the damn problem with Double
Doors? Traffic through Double Doors (and for that matter, on sidewalks) follows the exact same rules as Cars on a Road. Therefore,
Dear Reader, if you are in the United States, and are approaching
an entrance with Two Doors, then clearly, you should make for
the one on Your Right as you are Facing the Doors. People coming
from the Other Side of the Door will then pass through on Your
Left, and Pedestrian Traffic will be unimpeded. Under No Circumstances should you try to go through the left door, barreling into
Oncoming Crowds! Actually, the EGs would like to point out that
you *always* go through the door to Your Right, even if the door
to Your Left is Propped Open. It is not too much trouble for most
of us to Pull Open a Door, avoiding the start of an Annoying
Bottleneck.

Revolving Doors also seem to present a Big Problem for many
people. Again, just walk through them. You really *aren't* going to
get smooshed. The EGs get Particularly Annoyed when some
Timid Soul keeps making feeble efforts at stepping into the door,
causing a line of Other Pedestrians to form behind her. If you think
you'd like to Observe the Door before making that Big Move Into
It, then, Dear Reader, step to the side. Similarly, Escalators have
been around for a Good Long While, and you should be able to
step onto one without Five Minutes of Prep Time.

Small Children should be reigned in quite firmly when, as is
bound to happen, you cannot avoid taking them out in a Busy
Place. However, the EGs think this can be accomplished by simply
holding their hands. There is no reason you should even consider
going out in public avec more Small Children than you can easily
hold by the hand at one time. We do not approve of those leash-
type contraptions, as they are rather embarrassing for the poor

Small Children, who are not, we remind you, Small Pets; you should be ashamed of *yourself* if you think your child needs a leash. It is most unamusing, not to mention THOR (The Height of Rudeness), to allow your Small Child to throw rocks in public, particularly on a sidewalk, *particularly* at the Etiquette Grrls as they attempt to window-shop. No one should laugh at Small Children who do such nefarious things. Rather, one should Glare Fiercely at their parents, and especially if one has been formally introduced to them, to encourage them to Nip Such Rambunctious Behavior in the Bud.

When a Boy is walking with a Girl on a sidewalk, he should walk between her and the street. This is so that any Wayward Mud that should splash up from the wheels of a Wayward Truck will hit him instead of her, because, after all, Girls wear pretty, delicate, and often expensive clothing, which Wayward Mud would surely destroy. Furthermore, should the Wayward Truck or, horrors, a Wayward Bicycle, veer into the sidewalk, Boys are generally stronger and more threatening in appearance, and stand a better chance of deflecting the Wayward Vehicle, or at least absorbing the initial impact before the Wayward Vehicle runs into the Girl.

Pedestrians Versus Cars

Cars: Drivers of cars should, naturally, pay attention to Where the Pedestrians Are, and drive carefully around them. Pedestrians are not, in fact, on foot solely to Bother You or Impede Your Progress, and it will not hurt you to stop where you are supposed to and let them cross. Similarly, if a Pedestrian is crossing when a "Walk" sign is lit, and he is in a crosswalk, it is unnecessary for you to glare at him when he passes in front of Your Car. The EGs are certain the Pedestrian was not waiting for hours by the "Push Button for Walk Signal" Sign, poised for you to Drive Up so he could Make *You,* Yes, *You In Particular,* have to stop. So lighten up, Dear Reader. The EGs wouldn't know, but we hear Yoga is Calming.

Pedestrians: The cars are Bigger Than You. So watch out, and don't Try Anything Funny, like running halfway across the busy street and hanging out on the Double Yellow Line until traffic thins out on the other side. If the sign says "Don't Walk," and there's a Car Approaching, *DON'T FREAKIN' WALK.* Or at least, walk fast enough so that the oncoming car does not have to slow down or stop for you. While we're on the subject, if a car is nice enough to stop and let you go, especially when it is out of the Goodness of the Driver's Heart and not because he is just Obeying the Law Because There's a Cop Right There, you should make a concerted effort to cross the street without dawdling. The EGs hate waiting for people to look at the pretty buildings, stop and pet a puppy, wave hello to someone they recognize, answer their Cell 'Phone, etc. We would never begrudge anyone These Joys of Life, but we suggest you enjoy them on the Sidewalk, and not in the Middle of the Street. Of course, you should, as you trot across the street at a fast clip, wave Your Thanks to any Kind Driver who Stopped for You. Also, if you are Walking the Streets at Night (oh, Quit Your Snickering, Dear Reader, you know we don't mean it *that* way) it might be a good idea Not to Leap Out into Traffic if you're wearing All Black. Even if drivers are *supposed* to stop for you at a particular crosswalk, if they cannot see you, you cannot expect them to stop! The EGs understand the great joy it is to Slink Along in Head-to-Toe Black, but it would be smart of you to place a Nice Vintage Silver Pin on your coat's lapel, or to wear something else that Reflects a Bit of Light.

Also, if there is a Sidewalk Available, *USE IT!* Do not meander out into the Middle of the Road and then glare at cars for coming close to you—the cars, Dear Reader, *must* use the road. They have No Choice in the Matter. You, however, can walk perfectly well on the sidewalk. If there is no sidewalk, then, Dear Reader, you should stay as far away from traffic as possible.

Pedestrians should be Especially Cautious when walking in Another City. Sometimes Pedestrians have the Right of Way; sometimes They Don't. If you blithely wander into the road in London and expect that cars will stop for you, Dear Reader, you are Sorely Mistaken, and we bet you will be Pretty Sore.

BICYCLE ETIQUETTE

Bicycles are vastly overrated, the Etiquette Grrls believe, and are quite frequently the source of notorious rudeness on our streets. You should either live in a Neighborhood where you may walk to everywhere you need to be, or you should have a car at your disposal. Bicycles should only be used for rides in the country or in the Tour de France. However, if you insist upon using a bicycle in your town or city, you must observe the following rules.

Ride your bicycle in the road. The "cycle" in "bicycle" means that it, in fact, has wheels, and thus, belongs in the road, the province of All Things Wheeled. A sidewalk, we remind you, contains the word "walk," which means that only Pedestrians are allowed upon it.

You must ride at the very edge of Said Road. The Etiquette Grrls find it *extremely* irksome when a bicyclist has an inflated idea of his or her Personal Space. Clearly, if the Etiquette Grrls are driving around in the Etiquette Volvo, and you are merely on a bicycle, you should get the hell out of our way. You should not pedal slowly along, veering into the middle of the road, thus preventing the Etiquette Volvo from passing you safely and causing the Etiquette Grrls to wish it were polite to Mow You Down.

You should know, and use, Hand Signals to indicate your turns. You will, of course, look like an idiot doing this, but this is The Price You Pay for riding a bicycle in the first place.

No more than one person is allowed to ride a bicycle at one time. Tandem bicycles are quite silly, and anyone who is riding one appears to have gone off course from the Main Parade Route.

The bottom line: If you must ride a bicycle, the only acceptable type of bicycle is one that is Vintage and British and Rather Clunky, with a nice wicker basket attached to the handlebars. The image you must cultivate in order to get away with being on a bicycle is that of a studious Oxonian or Cantabrigian, sans, of course, the Academic Robes. You are not allowed to have a flashy neon bike, or to use a "mountain" or "dirt" bike in the city, where it is likely there are neither mountains nor dirt.

What You Should Wear While Riding a Bicycle

Don't wear a Miniskirt. Also, everything stated re: Pedestrians in Head-to-Toe Black above applies also to Bicyclists. Finally, it is imperative that you *not* wear so-called "bike" shorts. They are flattering to no one, and, Dear Reader, have we not made it clear that you should not be riding a bicycle so much or so far that you require a Specialized Costume?

SCOOTERS, SKATEBOARDS, AND INLINE SKATES

Maybe they're fun for Fourteen-Year-Old Boys, but if you're an Adult, you should not use any of these as a Mode of Transportation. We're perfectly fine with folks inline skating around the park for exercise, but if you're in your thirties and your conversational topics include "Backside 180 Ollies," and you have posters of Tony Hawk in your bedroom, you need to Reexamine Your Priorities. And no one over sixteen should be Caught Dead on a Skateboard or on one of those Razor Scooter Things.

VESPAS

Well, the EGs haven't an Awful Lot to Say about Vespas, except that we think they're Smashing and we each want one! We especially adore that Beautiful Pale Blue Shade they come in—it reminds us of Tiffany's Boxes! If the EGs only lived in a Warm Climate and didn't have to Travel Long Distances to get to most places, we could go *everywhere* on Our Matching Vespas! Vrrroom! Would anyone like to donate a Wee Palazzo in Florence to the EGs, to help us Realize Our Dream? We would send you the Most

Exquisitely Phrased Thank-You Note, on lovely, lovely paper . . . please?

Questions and Answers on Various and Sundry

Dearest Grrls de Etiquette,

Are Jell-O Moulds improper when entertaining high-profile guests like the Pope, the Queen of England, and People in General?

Whilst on the topic of food, how did marshmallows make their way into the Thanksgiving dinner circuit? Is this acceptable dinner fodder?

Also, is it in poor taste to run naked and screaming at prestigious and sacred places like Trinity College, Oxford; the Sistine Chapel at the Vatican; funerals and weddings; graduation ceremonies; and Disneyland? (Oh dear—Is it an etiquette faux pas to mention that place?)

Sincerely,
Le Duke of Denver

Your Grace,

Goodness! Aren't you just Full of Questions, Dear Duke! Let's start at the beginning: Jell-O is a Vile Thing, particularly when it has soggy slices of fruit or Wee Marshmallows mysteriously suspended inside it, defying gravity. Also, Jell-O reminds the Etiquette Grrls of School Cafeterias and Hospitals, neither of which ever offer a Pleasant Dining Experience. Furthermore, and perhaps more to the point, whatever it is that such places do offer in the way of Dining Experiences is probably something which you should not attempt to emulate at your own Dining Table. Not only is Jell-O an inappropriate item to serve to Dignitaries, but there is simply no proper way nor time to serve Jell-O, ever. Its very existence is best ignored.

Funny you should ask about marshmallows, Dear Duke. In fact, we were just wondering the very thing! Did the Pilgrims serve marshmallows at Plymouth? The Etiquette Grrls, although not

American History Experts, feel that we can safely say the answer is no. The Etiquette Grrls are Big On Tradition; hence, we really wish that people would stop insisting on serving marshmallows with Vegetables, which, prior to being encrusted avec the Silly Things, were Perfectly Respectable and Dignified. Particularly at Thanksgiving Dinner.

And lastly, although we are aware that *The Official Preppy Handbook* condones what is popularly referred to as "streaking," and, in fact, claims that such activities are Acceptable Preppy High-Jinks, the Etiquette Grrls Beg to Differ. We remind you, Dear Duke, that the Etiquette Grrls are not only From New England, but Catholic, and simply cannot even think of such things! In fact, the Etiquette Grrls firmly believe that everyone should remain Fully Clothed at All Times. Even when showering. And, oh, yes . . . You're quite right, the Etiquette Grrls refuse to acknowledge the existence of Disneyland, even though it is, by virtue of age, perhaps a trifle less appalling than Disney World. But still—trust us, Dear Duke. It will be a Cold Day in Hell before the Etiquette Grrls are seen at either place.

Yours faithfully,
The Etiquette Grrls

Dearest Etiquette Grrls,

A sister of one of my Very Close Friends is getting married. As I have spent time with the family at the Vineyard, I know the marrying sister quite well also. The wedding is a weekend affair, and I am unsure as to whether or not I can bring a date. The invitation did not specify. However, my friend said many months ago that it was fine to bring a date, but, and this is a big one, the family is Texan. Was she just being Texan, or is it really okay for me to bring a guest with me? On the reply card I wrote something like, "I am delighted to accept your invitation, and we look forward to seeing you at the Vineyard come June." A vague reply, I admit. "We" could refer to me and the friend I typically travel to the

Vineyard with (a wedding guest in a similar quandary). Or, "We" could refer to me in addition to my strangely animated fur cape. Who knows?

I know the whole family is madly planning The Wedding, and my friend, the sister of the bride, lives in Ecuador and is a trifle difficult to contact. How do I find out if I may bring a guest without making them feel obligated to say yes? I certainly don't want to take advantage of my friends' hospitality! Please Help!

Affectionately,
Invited, yet Unsure

Dear Invited,

Or perhaps they thought you meant "we" as in You and Your Travel Bar? Or peut-être they thought you meant "we" as in The Royal We? The Etiquette Grrls are Just Kidding, Dear Reader. The Etiquette Grrls know what you mean about Texans—Texans Think Big, and are quite often Very Welcoming and Big-Hearted, and are apt to adopt a "The More The Merrier" Attitude. Which is Marvelous. Unless, of course, you are a Hostess who ends up with A Hundred Uninvited Guests.

If the family is at all Kind, of course they will say that you may bring as many guests as you like, even if it is a Terrible Inconvenience for them, what with having to order more food, tables, etc. Therefore, Dear Reader, you, as a Good Friend to the Family In Question, should not put them in such a position. Further, the Etiquette Grrls remind you that a Wedding is a Gathering of the Bride's and Groom's Families and Very Close Friends on a Solemn Occasion, and it is in no way A Date. It is one thing to attend a Wedding as a Couple if you and your BF are both Family Friends of the Bride or Groom and have both been Invited. Or if you are An Established Couple—married, say—The Bride would, of course, invite you as A Couple, and this would have been Clearly Indicated on the Invitation. But if your Significant Other is a Complete Stranger to the Family, then there is really no reason for him to be there. In fact, wouldn't it all be Terribly Boring for BF, who knows No One? It's actually un peu cruel to subject the Poor Darling to The Whole Ordeal, is it not, Dear Reader? Moreover, and more importantly, it is Quite Jarring for the Poor Bride to, on this most Nerve-Wracking Occasion, spot an Interloper Skulking About. The Etiquette Grrls are sorry if this sounds harsh, but it's true. Just think, Dear Reader, how would you like it if you had spent months planning a Huge, Important Occasion down to the Finest Detail, and suddenly you were faced with Twice the Number of Guests you had planned for because everyone thought it would be okay to Bring a Sidekick? Not fun, Dear Reader, right? As the Old Publishing Adage goes, "when in doubt, leave it (or in this case, him) out."

Fondly,
The Etiquette Grrls

Dear Etiquette Grrls,

Is it proper to sneeze into the sleeve of your shirt while in public?

Sneezy

Dear Sneezy,

No! Nor in private!
Did you really think there was a Snowball's Chance in Hell that we would say yes? Just wondering,

The Etiquette Grrls

Dear Etiquette Grrls,

My lovely ladies, I am in a State of Confusion regarding Loud Music blaring from these so-called "Lowrider" cars in Southern California. Is it legal to blast Profanities on the street, particularly in the presence of youngsters and easily upset Elderly People? What, as a Respectable Cit-

izen, can I do? I have resorted to blasting my own music (from the cool swingy sounds of early Ol' Blue Eyes to the dramatic and elegant strains of Bach) over the sounds of these Thug-Mobiles, but feel as if I am not Beating Them, but rather Joining Them. Might we form a Task Force? Should we pester the Local Police about enforcing the noise pollution laws? As an Upstanding Citizen with Good Moral Virtues, and a Great Deal of Style and Taste (as well as a Fair Amount of Modesty), I wonder what I can do to prevent any senseless violence (on my part) regarding this situation?

Thank you, dear Etiquette Grrls.

I remain, your most humble and obedient servant, etc., etc.
Low Tolerance for Lowriders

Dear Low Tolerance,

We're afraid to report that the Atrocity that you describe is not limited to California—we've noticed the same Horrendous Abuse of car stereos everywhere, even, horrors, in Our Own Beloved New England. The Etiquette Grrls don't see any reason to ever subject others to such a racket! And we're Just Wondering why on earth anyone would need to play their music so loudly? The last time the Etiquette Grrls checked, there wasn't a need in This Country of Ours to announce, from miles away, Your Imminent Arrival at a particular point, in the manner of a Revolutionary War–Era Fife and Drum Corps. The Etiquette Grrls, like you, Dear Reader, have attempted to Drown Out the Offending Parties with our own music, but we, too, feel as if we're just Contributing to The Problem. We wouldn't recommend Voicing Your Opinion to the Offending Parties, though, as in These Sad, Sorry Days, the likelihood that you will Be Shot, or befall some other Dreadful Fate, seems rather high. In some towns, you could probably mount a Successful Campaign to get the Local P.D. to enforce the Noise-Pollution Laws, but in Big Cities, let's face it, The Fuzz keep themselves pretty well occupied with Robberies, Murders, and Wee Gang Wars. Your idea of Forming a Task Force is not a bad one, Dear Reader. Perhaps we can persuade Car Stereo Manufacturers to alter their products so that the volume cannot be raised above A Certain Level? In the meantime, Dear Reader, perhaps you should consider moving to a More Tranquil Part of Your Town.

Warm regards,
The Etiquette Grrls

CHAPTER TWO

"Where the Boys Are": Boys and Chivalric Behavior

The Etiquette Grrls think that Polite Boys are Really, Really Keen! Sadly, however, there are not enough of them, so we are Setting About to Correct Things! Why are the Polite Boys so few and far between? The EGs think there are probably two causes. First, in this Day and Age, nearly everyone has become Clueless and Lazy about Etiquette. And second, we think it is quite likely that many Boys are afraid of the Response They'll Get from Girls if they dare to Display Chivalry! Boys, no reasonable person is going to smack you over the head with a hefty volume of Simone de Beauvoir if you open a door for a Lady, or give up your seat on the bus to the Pregnant Woman. The Etiquette Grrls think it is Imperative that we each do our part to Correct This. Boys, stop being afraid to Be Chivalric! Girls, if a Boy holds a door for you, say Thank You, don't give him a Nasty Look! If you are on a sidewalk and he walks on the side Closer to the Street, don't ask, "What the hell are you doing?" If a Work Colleague happens to comment that you look nice today, don't Slug Him! (Unless he's truly Being Sleazy.

But honestly, Dear Girl, you should be Smart Enough to know the difference between a Simple Compliment and a Lascivious Comment, rather than assuming *All* Compliments are Lascivious.) We hope this section helps Boys become More Polite, and helps Girls realize how Polite Boys Behave.

The Elements of Chivalry

Yes, lots of these things may seem Un Peu Outdated to Your Post-Post-Modern Ears. However, that doesn't mean that you shouldn't be doing them! Vintage Clothing is by its very nature Outdated, too, and the EGs still wear it with pride! And we are Quite Bored avec the argument of, "If I don't understand *why* it's customary, I don't have to do it." That is just Laziness disguised as Semantics, Dear Reader. Why do Boys have to Remove Their Hats Indoors? The only reason you need is, "Because the EGs Said So."

- Polite Boys stand when a Girl enters the Room, and when she departs. Actually, everyone, regardless of Gender, should stand when An Elder, or A Very Important Person, enters or leaves.

- Boys should Open Doors for Girls. Please actually *hold* the door for the Girl, instead of merely flinging it open and running through, leaving her to Sprint Through Before It Slams. Open the door and step to the side while the Girl passes through (perhaps saying, "After you," if she hesitates). At this point, the Girl should politely thank the Boy. He then says, "You're welcome," and, when she is through the door, goes through it himself. See, Dear Reader, this is really Quite Simple!

- Girls precede Boys through every door except Revolving Doors. Boys, if you encounter a Revolving Door when you are walking with a Girl, you should enter it first so that you may Push the Door. (Of course, you should not push it Too

Fast, so that the Girl has to leap like a Gazelle to enter the Revolving Door you've set Spinning Out of Control.)

- Boys graciously Give Up Their Seats on buses, trains, etc., when all the seats are taken and a Girl is Forced to Stand. Simply say, "Excuse me, please take my seat." He should also offer to assist her with her luggage, especially if she is obviously attempting to heave her heavy Pullman Suitcase onto the awkwardly placed luggage rack. (Girls, of course, should immediately thank the Boy for His Kindness.) Again, the same principle applies to when the Elderly, the Infirm, the Obviously Frail, or the Pregnant are standing, no matter your, or their, gender.

- It is very nice for a Boy to Help a Girl into Her Coat. Just stand behind her and hold the coat by the shoulders while she puts her arms into it. There is no need, however, for you to Button It Up for Her, or help her on with her Mittens.

- In a Bar, if there is no Table Service, it's nice for the Boy to fetch the Drinks.

- Very Old-Fashioned, Polite Boys sometimes order for a Girl in a Restaurant. Now, if you're going to do this, you should inquire what the Girl would like to eat before placing the order with the Waitress. It would be very bad for her to have to correct you because she breaks out in Terrible Hives when she Eats Shrimp, for example. Also, you really have to be a Traditional, Perfectly Chivalric Boy to pull this off with grace, since your waiter at, say, Bennigan's probably isn't going to Expect It.

- If a Boy has asked a Girl out on a Date, he should Pay. This is just the Polite Thing to Do. If for some reason the Girl has Done the Asking, then the responsibility of paying is hers.

Under no circumstances should anyone on a First Date, reach for the check and demand that the Other Party pay up! In longer-term relationships, you may find yourselves Switching Off occasionally, as both parties will be Making Plans, and this is fine. The EGs just think it's nicer to alternate than to have both of you Reaching for Your Wallets every single time you go out.

- When you are taking seats at a Theater, Concert Hall, Movie Theater, Church, Lecture Hall, etc., the Girl precedes the Boy into the Row of Seats. In a Restaurant, when the Maître d' is leading you to your table, the Girl precedes the Boy.

- When a Girl is taking a seat at a Table, the Boy pulls out her chair for her. This is a Maneuver that takes a bit of practice to be done gracefully, however. (The EGs have heard Embarrassing Stories of Teenage Boys who know they should do this at, par exemple, the Prom, but get a bit Over-Zealous and yank the chair completely out from underneath Their Poor Dates. Not a Pretty Picture, Dear Reader.)

- Boys, take off the Damn Hats Indoors! For the record, no, Baseball Hats are not Exempt From This. Even if your hair is Quite Messy, you aren't allowed to Keep Your Hat on Indoors to hide it. And by "Indoors," we mean Anywhere With a Roof Over Your Head. There is no difference between leaving Your Hat on in the Grocery Store and in Your Parents' House.

- While we're on the subject of Hats, if you must wear a Baseball Cap when you are not Actually Playing Baseball or Watching a Baseball Game, at least wear it with the brim facing forward, the way it's supposed to be worn. Wearing it backward or, worse, with the brim Off to the Side, doesn't look cool or jaunty. It looks Ridiculous, as if Your Head Weren't On Straight.

- And another thing: *THROW OUT THE RATTY BASEBALL CAPS!* The EGs don't care if that dirty, sweat-stained, threadbare cap has Sentimental Value for You, we don't want to see it on Your Head! If it means that much to you, well, you shouldn't have let it Get Ratty in the First Place. Put it Out of Its Misery, please.

- If a Girl is carrying Something Unwieldy, or Something Heavy, or is Struggling in Any Manner with a Physical Task (such as Changing a Tire), it is kind of you to assist her. However, do ask first ("May I help you with that?" suffices) instead of just wresting the Giant Suitcase out of Her Hands, lest she think you are trying to Rob Her.

- If it is Raining, it is nice if the Boy holds the Umbrella if he is sharing it avec a Girl. (However, if the Girl is taller than he is, she may suggest that she hold it, so as to avoid being Unpleasantly Poked in the Eye.)

- If a Boy and a Girl are Walking Down the Sidewalk, the Boy walks on the side Closest to the Street. More on this on page 23.

- Let's say you are hanging out with Your College Buddies in a Bar. You've Tossed Back a Few, and are having a lively conversation. Now the EGs understand that Boys seem to think it is permissible to use, let's say, Rougher Language, and to have a Bit More Tolerance for particular kinds of Crude Humor when they are Around Other Boys. We do not, of course, approve of this! We want the Boys to be On Their Best Behavior at all times! Wouldn't you be Terribly Embarrassed if the Girl you've had a crush on for months walks by your table as you're participating in a Belching Contest? Well, Dear Boy, you should be Quite Embarrassed Indeed! Therefore, we encourage you to act as if Ladies Were Present everywhere you

go . . . it will undoubtedly result in more Ladies actually want-
ing to Spend Time With You.

- An Important Point: Boys are not excused from observing certain Principles of Etiquette just because they're Boys. Yes, you
must write Thank-You Notes, and bring Hostess Gifts, and
write Bread-and-Butter Letters. The Etiquette Grrls have quite
a problem with the opinion that paying attention to these
matters is something "only for Girls." How ridiculous!

- Chivalric Boys open Car Doors for Girls, also. Please note that
we do *not* mean simply pushing the Power Locks button to
unlock the door, or reaching across the front seat to open the
door for a Passenger. Full details may be found on page 14 in
our discussion of Driving Automobiles Politely.

- If it is Cold Out, it is very kind of you to offer Your Coat to
a Girl. (We do mean a Girl you know, of course; you wouldn't
want to go offering Your Nice Cashmere Overcoat to a Total
Stranger on the Subway, because you'd be Kissing It Good-
bye.) Let's say you and Your Date have just finished dinner at
a restaurant and need to walk several blocks to the Movie
Theatre. Inexplicably, the temperature has dropped thirty degrees whilst you were dining, and Your Date's Cashmere
Twinset isn't providing her much protection from the Cold.
She's shivering uncontrollably. If you're wearing a Sports Coat,
you should offer it to her. Naturally, the EGs think a Girl
should listen to the Weather Forecast before planning her outfit, and it's always better to bring a coat you don't need than
find yourself sans one, but Wee, Unexpected Cold Fronts do
occasionally take us all by surprise. If the Boy can tolerate the
Cold himself, it's nice of him to give his coat to the Girl. Of
course, if by giving up his coat he'd put himself in danger of
Frostbite, or, worse, Freezing to Death, the best thing to do
would be to Hail a Cab instead of Walking.

- Speaking of Cabs, it's Quite Chivalric for a Boy to leave enough money with the driver to cover the Girl's Cab Fare if the Boy is the first person to be Dropped Off. Also, if there is a group of three Girls and one Boy all sharing a cab, the Boy should be the one to Sit in Front avec the driver.

- If Boys are present at an event that features Dancing (e.g., a Wedding Reception, a College Formal, etc.), they should take it upon themselves to ensure that all Girls who would like to Dance make an appearance on the Dance Floor. Do not, under any circumstances, allow the Girls to congregate on one side of the room while the Boys stand on the other! If you are out of Middle School, this is Not Acceptable Behavior. Do you think the Girls have Cooties or something? You're not asking one of them to Marry You, you're simply spending three minutes or so Dancing With Her. Another thing about Dancing—it is totally and completely Charming for a Boy to know how to Dance. So few of them do! The EGs think this is probably Best Taken Care of when Boys are Quite Young, so they can go off to College with a secure knowledge of the Basic Fox-Trot, etc., but it wouldn't hurt for Boys of any age to take a few Ballroom- or Swing-Dancing Lessons so they can be Chivalric at Weddings and Formals.

- If a Boy and a Girl are at a Restaurant, and they decide to share a Bottle of Wine, it is proper for the Boy to order the Wine, taste it, etc. This is not to say that the Boy and the Girl shouldn't discuss what type of Wine they should get, but ideally the Boy would deal with the Sommelier. Don't be frightened by this. The Sommelier will present the Bottle to you so that you may Read the Label and ascertain that this is, in fact, the Wine You Ordered. (If anything is Incorrect, point it out to the Sommelier: "I'm sorry, but I believe I ordered the '98, not the '99.") The Sommelier will uncork the bottle and will present you with the Cork. Contrary to Popular Belief, this is not so you can Smell It. This is so you can look at it and make sure it's not Crumbled or Moldy or otherwise Abnormal in Appearance. In most cases, the Cork will be Just Fine. The Sommelier will then pour a bit of the Wine into your glass. Taste it, but please don't affect "wine-tasting behaviors" in any kind of Pretentious Way, as you are not actually at a Wine Tasting, you are In a Restaurant. Take a sip, and make sure it doesn't taste "off" in any way. (If you simply Don't Like the Wine, this is Rather Unfortunate, but you're stuck with the bottle unless something is actually Wrong With It. It would behoove you to ask the Sommelier before you order if you're not sure a Wine is sweet or dry, for example.) If the Wine tastes acceptable, tell the Sommelier that it's good, and allow him to pour it for you and Your Date.

- If you're Pouring Wine or Serving Drinks, serve the Girls first.

- Boys should light Cigarettes for Girls. A Boy should also, before smoking, inquire if the Girl minds if he smokes, and then offer her a cigarette before taking one himself. Naturally, he lights her cigarette first, too. For good examples of How This Is Done elegantly, watch a few Old Movies.

The EGs would also like to say that one is Chivalric because one is a Good Person who genuinely wants to Make the World a More Polite Place. It is horrible to *pretend* to be Chivalric when in fact one has Ulterior Motives! You are not allowed to expect the Girl you assisted with her luggage will Go On a Date With You, and you are most certainly not allowed to send someone a Bill for Helping Her Change Her Tire! The only thing you should expect to receive in return for a Chivalric Act is a pleasant, sincere "Thank You." And once you have said, "You're Welcome," you both may be on Your Merry, Polite Ways.

One last thing: Do be aware that in this Day and Age, Girls absolutely must be Un Peu Suspicious of Strange Boys when they encounter them in an Isolated Setting. If a Girl's Car breaks down on a desolate street with no streetlamps on a Moonless Night, it is lovely of you to want to Assist Her, but please understand that she is probably Already Frightened to be Stranded. In this case, please do not be surprised or offended if she does not Get Out of Her Car. The best thing you could say in this situation would probably be, "Do you need any help? I'd be happy to telephone the Police, or a towing service." Believe the EGs, Girls *hate* that we have to be So Suspicious, but, sadly, there are too many Creeps Out There for us to be completely trustful of Strangers when We're Alone.

Style for Boys

To say that the EGs don't care for Jewelry on Boys would be a Grand Understatement. A Wedding Band is appropriate, as is a Watch, and perhaps Cuff Links. Anything additional is simply too much. Under no circumstances should Boys wear Gold Chains (particularly Lots of Them at Once, à la Mr. T, unless, of course, you *are* Mr. T, in which case we'll let it slide), Bracelets, or any sort of Brooch! We don't like Earrings too much, either, but, Dear Boys, if you are going through some sort of Earring Phase, then for God's Sake, keep the Earrings very, very simple. You should definitely steer clear of Diamond Studs, anything Dangly, and, for the Love of God, any sort of Pearls. Fortunately, the EGs have never seen a Boy wearing a Clip-On Earring, but this also would look Quite Ridiculous. We tend to think that most Boys with earrings look like they think they're Pirates, especially if they're wearing Hoops. Let's leave that look to Captain Hook, shall we, Lads?

The Etiquette Grrls have noticed (perceptive sorts that we are) that Boys, in general, seem to have a Morbid Fear of Irons. It is not enough simply to fold one's clothes when they emerge from the Dryer—usually, they are Still Wrinkled, and if you plan on Leaving Your Apartment, anything you wear must be Neatly Pressed. We would like to offer Our Endorsement of some of the Fabulous Non-Iron Shirts and Pants available at Brooks Brothers, however! These look Smashing, and because they exist, you have No Excuse to wear Wrinkly Khakis out in public.

Please purchase some Plain, White T-Shirts and wear them under your Button-Down Shirts. You may be wearing the Most Lovely, Elegantly Cut, White Button-Down Shirt from Thomas Pink, but if your T-Shirt's inscription of "New England Patriots Super Bowl Champs 2002!!!" shows through, your Entire Appearance is Ruined. In fact, you must wear a T-shirt, period—especially if the Weather is Hot. (And if the weather is cold, Dear Boy, why wouldn't you, for Extra Warmth?)

In many ways, Boys are very lucky, in that Men's Fashion does not veer off into Ridiculous Trends quite as easily as Women's. If, however, it does do this for some reason, Do Not Follow It! If the Gap told you to Jump Off a Bridge, would you do it? Boys should not be wearing Cropped Pants, Ridiculously Baggy Pants, Tank Tops, Camouflage Print (unless, of course, they are Actual Members of Our Armed Forces), Velour Powder-Blue Sweatsuits, Bowling Shirts (unless they are, in fact, Bowling), Ski Hats in Summer, etc. Also, in the EGs' Expert Opinion, there is no need whatsoever for any Boy to sport a Bizarre Haircut, Bizarre Highlights, Bizarre Sideburns, Bizarre Facial Hair, etc. If a hairstyle has been invented anytime in, say, the past thirty years, it's probably not the Best Look for you. And we have Had It Up to Here with the Stupid Goatees/Soul Patches/Flavor Savers/What Have You. (Dear God, "Soul Patches"? "Flavor Savors"?? A good rule: If it's got an idiotic name like that, it doesn't belong On Your Face.) No, for your information, it is *not* a requirement that if you are In College, you must grow some Wacky Facial Hair. If you really do believe that you look best with a Beard or a Mustache or a Simple Goatee, please keep it Neatly Groomed. If you do not have a Beard or a Mustache or a Simple Goatee, then Go Shave! Right Now! The EGs don't approve of Fuzzy, Unkempt Stubble, either. We like clean-shaven Boys, no arguments about it!

Now, there is no need for you to Go Get a Manicure every

week like the EGs do, but trust us, it really won't kill you to keep
your nails looking nice. Clip or file them regularly, and use a good
hand lotion to keep them Looking Their Best. The same thing goes
for Your Feet, if you plan to be spending any time at a Beach or
Pool.

As for those troublesome Receding Hairlines: oh, you Poor Boy!
The EGs know this causes Much Consternation in Boys who ex-
perience it, especially when they are Quite Young. But honestly,
Dear Reader, a Receding Hairline is nothing to be embarrassed
about. What is embarrassing, however, is the variety of Obvious,
Ineffective Attempts at disguising hair loss. If you have one piece
of hair that is eight inches long that you arrange into an Intricate
Spiral Pattern over the entire hairless crown of your head, no one
is going to Buy It. And please, for the Love of God, do not get
Hair Plugs! They are so terribly easy to spot! Or, worse, a Cheap
Toupee! Really, Dear Reader, just go to a Good Barber and let him
give you a Flattering Haircut that does not involve Combovers.

Makeup on Boys: No. *NO NO NO NO NO!* Unless, of course, it
is Halloween (and you are dressed as, say, Robert Smith, or Boy
George, or a member of KISS), or you are An Actor who is currently on stage or filming.

How to Buy Beautiful Flowers

It is Simply Charming when a Boy arrives at a Girl's Door with a
Lovely Bouquet in Hand! However, we have noticed that many
Boys are intimidated by Florists' Shops. We understand; they must
be Utterly Foreign Territory, as Florists' Shops are Flowery and
Frilly and Smell Divine—quite the opposite of Your Average Boy's
Apartment! Yet you need not be afraid, especially if you follow the
EGs' Advice.

First, do not resort to those Nationwide Floral Delivery Services.
If we might be permitted An Analogy, their arrangements are Store-
Bought Chips Ahoy Cookies, while arrangements obtained from a
Neighborhood Florist are Gooey, Warm, Homemade Cookies. Un-

derstood? If you are ever sending flowers From a Distance, always call a Reputable Florist in the Recipient's City. You will want to inquire about what kinds of flowers are Particularly Good on That Day before specifying what type of bouquet or arrangement you want. You may have been thinking of Pink Roses, but if the florist says he has Spectacular Gardenias, while the Pink Roses are still kind of Tightly Closed Buds, you would be wise to go with the Gardenias. Also ask in what type of container, if any, the flowers will be delivered. We advise erring on the side of Simplicity here. Do not allow the florist to talk you into Cutesy, "Country"-ish painted vases, or anything with a Holiday Theme, or anything accompanied by Balloons, Pom-Poms, a Teddy Bear, or Plastic Signs. A Plain Glass Vase is much preferable. If you are unable to locate a Reputable Florist in the Recipient's City, as much as we loathe to say it, Martha Stewart's online catalogue has a beautiful selection of flowers which may be purchased and delivered by the bunch, with or without a vase. Furthermore, Martha being Martha, you *know* that she's not going to allow anyone to bring you a bunch of half-dead red carnations and baby's breath instead of the lovely pale-pink roses you ordered, seeing as nobody, not even FedEx, dares to defy Martha!

If you are picking up flowers yourself, or having them delivered locally, do Take Courage and venture into the Florist Shop. You can ask the same questions there, and even see the Very Flowers that will go into the bouquet or arrangement.

Always remember that Beautiful Flowers do not need to be Exorbitantly Expensive. An armful of Pretty Daisies or Daffodils or whatever happens to be in season is Always Lovely. All the Girls the EGs know would much prefer a bouquet like that to some sort of Wacky, Nouveau Arrangement containing One Weird Orchid and Some Sort of Thorny Seaweed. The EGs aren't too keen on arrangements with Carnations (particularly Dyed Carnations) or Lilies, which seem Un Peu Funereal to us, but if you know that the Girl just adores White Lilies, then you may go ahead and buy them for her. A Very Smart, Perceptive Boy will Pay Attention to what kinds of flowers the Object of His Affection loves and hates. If she calls your attention to flowers, listen! "Oh, look at the beautiful Irises! They are my Very Favorite Flower!" is Important Information, Dear Boy! Similarly, "Yeccch, I simply *despise* Peonies," or, "I'm terribly allergic to Roses," is something to Make a Mental Note Of. Also be sure to note the décor of her flat. Is everything predominately Shades of Pink? Then Red Roses or Orange Tiger Lilies are going to look horrid, no matter how lovely the flowers themselves are. Don't be afraid to tell the florist, "I'd like a simple arrangement all in shades of pink and white, please."

Finally, if you are having the flowers delivered, you should compose a Short Message to accompany them. Try to go for "Sweet, but Not Embarrassing." And be sure to sign your damn name, too. The EGs hate it when a Mystery Bouquet arrives at Our Door, saying only, "Happy Birthday," and we think, in a moment of insanity, that we have a Mystery Admirer, or that Harry Connick, Jr., *finally* remembered Our Birthday, but then we find out that they were only from the Etiquette Mom. (Not that we're ungrateful, or anything, but sometimes, one gets one's hopes up, you know.)

Charming, Yet Inexpensive, Ideas for Dates

- **A Picnic.** We know this sounds Trite, but it's Still Fun. Even if you're not a Gourmet Chef, you can put together a nice basket of drinks and snacks. A bottle of wine, a box of Carr's Crackers, a few different kinds of cheese, and some Bartlett Pears would make for a Wonderful Picnic!

- **Minor-League Baseball Games.** Most Girls aren't too keen on Sports, it's true, but on a Nice Day, it can be a Smashing Lot of Fun to go to a Baseball Game, even if we don't follow the team. It just seems very All-American.

- **Almost Any Kind of Museum.** Well, maybe that Medical Oddities Museum in Philadelphia wouldn't be a great choice if your date is a Bit Queasy, but a Local Historical Museum, a small Sculpture Garden, or a Restored Home that offers tours all promise a very interesting afternoon, even if you can't get to New York to go to The Met.

- **Apple-picking.** Provided, of course, that it is a Nice Day and no one is Afraid of Heights. (Add that Extra-Special Touch and Memorize the Frost Poem!)

- **Anywhere you went on a Field Trip as a Child.** It's likely to be either Far More Interesting than you remember it being, or, conversely, Cheesy as All Hell, both of which Have Their Joys.

- **A Flea Market or Antiques Fair.** There's lots of Neat Stuff to Look At, lots of Amusing Junk, and you can talk about it all for Hours.

- **Fireworks Displays.** Okay, so these don't Happen Terribly Often, but they do make for a Fun Date. As long as it's not Freezing Cold, or Raining, etc., and the Fireworks are being set off by Professionals. A couple of Quarter Sticks and Some Matches does *not* equal a Pleasant Evening.

- **Find a Map.** Pick a town within Driving Distance that neither of you has Ever Visited. Go there and Investigate.

- Is there, say, **a Very Famous Small Ice-Cream Shop** an hour's drive away? Take a Mini Road Trip!

- **A group ballroom- or swing-dancing class.** If you can dance already, Dear Boy, your date will be Extremely Impressed. If you can't, she'll think you're the Bee's Knees for Trying!

Dates You Shouldn't Go On

The Etiquette Grrls often find ourselves Besieged by Clever, Handsome, Witty Boys from Good Families ringing us up to ask if we would care to accompany them on Various Jaunts about town. In fact, this occurs *so* often, and all the Boys are of *such* an Exemplary Character, that we are forced to Narrow The Choices Down by the activities that are offered. Everyone knows what sort of activities are acceptable to the Etiquette Grrls—for instance, in addition to the above-listed suggestions, lunch at Tavern On The Green, a Sinatra concert at The Sands (okay, so that would involve some time-travel, but whatever), or a screening of *Rear Window* are all, obviously, excellent choices. But where, you ask, *shouldn't* you go on a date? For Quick and Easy Reference, we provide you, Dear Reader, with A List of Places That You Should Avoid while on a date. (Most *especially* on a First Date.) This list naturally is not all-inclusive, but we hope you'll get the idea.

- **Andrew Lloyd Webber Musicals.** True Theatre Aficionados like the Etiquette Grrls look at such Blight on the Theatrical World with scorn, and firmly believe that you shouldn't go to one of these Monstrous Productions, *ever*. (See page 96)

- **Monster-Truck Rallies.** The Etiquette Grrls shouldn't have to explain this to their Dear Readers.

- **Any Professional Wrestling Event.** Again, if we have to tell you why you shouldn't be there, you are Beyond Help.

- **An NRA Convention.** Conventions are boring. The NRA is scary. This is not a good combo, especially on a date. If you're a Charlton Heston fan, we suggest you rent videos of his films and watch them from the safety of your own home.

- **Exhibition Gymnastic or Skating Competitions.** Boring, boring, boring. Tacky, tacky, tacky. Pointless, pointless, pointless.

You'd be better off going to see something with *real* dance numbers, like *Cabaret*.

- **The Shooting Range.** Unless you *really* don't like your date, and are interested in demonstrating what will happen if he or she doesn't Shape Up, Stat! But, really, this seems Rather Unnecessary and just a Tad Overbearing.

- **Any Sort of Interpretive Dance Production.** Again, you Just Plain Shouldn't Be Here. It's Pretentious, and Silly, and Awful. No one *really* likes Interpretive Dance Numbers. C'mon. Admit it.

- **Your Group Therapy Session.** A bad, bad, bad idea. Do you really want Your Date to find out All Your Dirt right off the bat like that? Moreover, the Etiquette Grrls feel that Group Therapy is Rather Tacky under any circumstances, as it tends to encourage loud, messy expressing of one's Emotions in front of Strangers. The Etiquette Grrls are From New England, and, therefore, are Staunchly Against such behavior, and are Rather Suspicious of people who actually seem to enjoy this sort of thing.

- **Any Sort Of *Star Trek* or *X-Files* Convention or Other Gathering.** Watching *The X-Files* is cool. *X-Files* conventions are not. If you have to go somewhere expressly to meet other people who avidly watch the Adventures of Agents Mulder and Scully in syndication, you really need to Get Out More. If you spend gabillions of dollars on Action Figures, Comic Books, and Other Paraphernalia, you're *really* on a Dangerous Road, and should, perhaps, Seek Help. And this is probably Not The Best Impression that you could give on a First Date. Ditto for anything to do with *Star Trek*, which in the Etiquette Grrls' opinion, isn't even as cool as *X-Files* anyway.

- **Def Con.** See comments about conventions, above. Plus, Def Con is now *much* too Pop Culture, and there are all sorts of uncool hangers-on and groupies floating about. Besides, who wants to go to Vegas in the Middle of the Summer? If you and your date are Really *Mad* for "Computer Security" conferences, try SummerCon instead.

Questions and Answers on Various and Sundry

Dear Etiquette Grrls,

I've recently found myself thrust back into the Dating Game and though I think my hand Flush, all of my friends want me to Bluff! The Sitch is an old story, but I cannot find the happy ending. While managing to date, casually and simultaneously, several young men, I fall for one in particular. Typically, Mr. Particular pays me the least attention. He is every inch a gentleman and sometimes this translates into reserved behavior. Of course, the others call all of the time.

Is it fair to be wined and dined by the Second Runner-Up whilst you are mooning over Bachelor Number One? What if the Second Suitor is a cad or, even worse, a Total Bore? Isn't it even more misleading to continue to see him just to pass the time? Not to mention masochistic? Might it be reasonable in such circumstances to invent a Dashing Companion, thereby seeming as in demand as one may actually be, and yet not forcing one's self to Suffer Fools?

Please help! My friends rely too much on The Rules *to be counted on for good advice.*

Yours Sincerely,
Miss Monogamy

Dear Miss Monogamy,

The Etiquette Grrls entirely sympathize with Your Plight. Boys are, to generalize, A Problem. The Etiquette Grrls particularly Feel

Your Pain regarding Suitor Number One, the reserved type. It seems that, in recent memory, we have had to spend entirely too many days e-mailing each other, regarding similarly wonderful yet reserved boys, wondering when the Agony would end.

It is, in the Etiquette Grrls' opinion, peut-être un peu masochiste to see Suitors one has No Great Interest In, not to mention perhaps just the Teensiest Bit Unfair to said Unsuitable Suitors. Probably this is time Best Spent in a local bar Tossing Back a Few with Your Best Friends, who, surely, know you very well, know Suitor Number One, and will do Anything In Their Power to get the boy to Come To His Senses. Perhaps it is best if you do not actually invent a Dashing Companion to whom you yourself frequently refer (probably not the sort of lie one would relish being caught in); however, certainly, you could count on your Closest Friends to tell Suitor Number One about how wonderful you and your social life are. The Etiquette Grrls themselves would be more than happy to Take Up Your Cause, should we ever encounter The Gentleman In Question.

In general, the Etiquette Grrls think that it would be Most Helpful if Boys would just Declare Their Intentions, Already, thereby eliminating the Messy State of our Pining Away after them. The Etiquette Grrls know this would be A Bold Step, Dear Reader, and would perhaps require More Courage than we ourselves possess, but have you considered Directly Asking Suitor Number One about your relationship? Perhaps he is unsure of how you feel about him, and is simply being cautious—rather a nice contrast to the Myriad Random Idiots who attempt to impress Nice Girls with their pseudo-suave advances. He may be very glad you took the initiative; *The Rules,* once again, and as always, can See the Etiquette Grrls In Hell over this one. Dear Reader, we wish you The Best of Luck! Let us know what happens!

Hang in there,
The Etiquette Grrls

Dear Etiquette Grrls,

I am an Older Man, and I was wondering what the best way to approach a significantly younger woman would be. For instance, girls ignore me if I just introduce myself, but my friends tell me that faking a coronary in the middle of a Sorority Party might be going a little too far. Tell me, Etiquette Grrls, where is one to draw the line?

Approaching Retirement

Dear Approaching,

Eeeeew. Dear Reader, the Etiquette Grrls respectfully suggest that you only attempt to date within your Age Group. The Etiquette Grrls strongly disapprove of Trophy Brides. We remind you that your girlfriend/wife should never, ever, ever be mistaken for Your Daughter, or, horrors, Your Granddaughter. Not only is this In Poor Taste, but it is most embarrassing for all involved, especially Your Actual Daughter or Granddaughter, should she, in fact, exist.

Sincerely,
The Etiquette Grrls

Dear Etiquette Grrls,

I was convinced that I would never be writing to you again. I had solved The Boy Problem, you see, by swearing them off. No contact, no quandary! I have come to learn, of course, that we can only control our own actions, if even those.

As soon as I decided never to chase down a man again, I became a Hot Commodity—to men who have girlfriends whom I know slightly. Why can they never get these things right? Jerks. The question is what to do with this information. I do not know the girlfriends well enough for heart-to-heart chats—I have informed select mutual friends, but they intend to say nothing. I am content to keep quiet, but how do I nip these

Flirtatious Forays in the bud without disrupting an entire Social Set?
Color me unused to this side of betrayal.

Aidez-moi!

Sincerely,
Miss Monogamy

P.S. I saw Bachelor Number One this weekend, who, as you know,
has Forgotten That I Exist. Predictably he didn't say a word to me, and
I got so furious that I began to twitch all over. I thought about marching
up to him, punching him in the face, on purpose this time, and saying,
"You won't forget about me now, #$*%!" But, in a surprise move I
showed restraint. It was a good idea, I concluded, but a bad thing to
actually do. Are you terribly proud?

Dear Miss Monogamy,

The Etiquette Grrls send you their best regards and are so happy
to hear from you again! First, let us congratulate you on your
Excellent Behavior avec Bachelor Number One! We are constantly
reining ourselves in from smacking Those Who Have Wronged Us,
and we feel that such restraint should be commended, nay, cele-
brated. Trust us, Dear Reader, there would be an awful lot of Sorry
People if everyone who had trifled with the Etiquette Grrls or Our
Dear Friends got a Swift Kick in the Shins. But we continue to
attempt to conduct ourselves with Grace and Dignity, and we are
indeed Terribly Proud of your doing the same, Dear Reader! But
on to your first question. How horrible, Miss Monogamy! For
shame on those Horrid Men! Quels Dastardly Bastards and Shameless Cads! The Etiquette Grrls have found that deftly chosen comments reminding the fellow of his girlfriend tend to work Rather
Well in such situations . . . "Your upcoming trip to Newport sounds
exciting. Will (insert name of girlfriend here) be able to accompany
you?" "I'm looking forward to (insert name of mutual friend)'s
party. Are you and (insert name of girlfriend) planning to go?" We

suggest you do this often enough (perhaps merely Pointedly enough would suffice) to let them know You're Onto Them. Your mutual friends might drop similar hints. Good luck, Miss Monogamy!

All will be well,
The Etiquette Grrls

CHAPTER THREE

"I'm Gonna Sit Right Down and Write Myself a Letter": Letters for All Occasions

Review: Supplies

As we wrote in *Things You Need to Be Told*, it is of the utmost importance that if you are going to Write a Letter (as well you should), you must, like the Boy Scouts, Be Prepared. This means not just knowing What to Say, and How to Say It, but to have a Writing Desk, full of Supplies. In brief, here are some of the Things You Will (and Will Not) Need Before you sit down to Write a Good Letter.*

- Good paper. White or Ecru. Possibly Light Blue or Grey. The Etiquette Grrls feel that one can never go wrong with Crane's paper, but you should simply avail yourself of the nicest and plainest paper you can afford, keep lots on hand, and you will never be forced to write A Condolence Note on sunshine-yellow paper with an ink glitter pen.

- Real Paper: No backs of grocery lists/receipts, 1,000 of the wee-est Post-its, etc. (See above.)

- If Your Paper is personalized, choose a normal font and normal ink. No cute designs or wacky colors allowed.

- Real ink. Fountain or rollerball. Black, blue, or blue-black only. Pencil, crayon, marker, highlighter, nailpolish, ink from Cheapo, Skippy Ballpoint Pens, and erasable ink are not acceptable.

- Legible handwriting. Well, it's a Nice Plus, anyway.

- Nice Stamps. While it's true that any ol' stamp will get your letter from Point A to Point B, it's not always true that a Stamp is a Stamp is a Stamp. Our Post Office offers a Wide Variety of stamps at any given time, and for Nice Letters, it's often a Good Finishing Touch to use a Pretty Non-Standard Stamp instead of a regular Flag Stamp. (Not that we don't like Flag Stamps, no siree, Bob!)

Supplies You Do Not Need

- Confetti

- Stickers, unless writing to a small child; or they're plain gold, silver, or clear seals for the back of the envelope, especially if the envelope n'a pas de glue, which sometimes happens with Expensive, Imported Handmade Paper.

- Pre-printed return address labels, which are only okay for informal correspondence and paying bills, but not Important Things like Your Wedding Invitations or Formal Letters to The President.

The Standard Thank-You Note

You must write thank-you notes for everything, always, Dear Reader! It'll only take a minute! Here's an example of a basic thank-you note:

September 1, 2005

Dear Katherine,

Thank you so much for the wonderful book about nineteenth-century architecture of Long Island that you sent me. Not only was it the perfect present (I haven't been able to put it down!), but it will certainly come in handy for my studies. You always pick the perfect thing!

Again, thanks so much, and I'll talk to you soon.

Love,
Bitsy

The Horribly Belated Thank-You Note

See above. Make no mention of the fact that your note is six months late. Regardless of the excuse you give, you will sound like you're lying.

The Thank-You Note for the Unwanted

At some point, you will, without doubt, receive a gift which you will hate and/or Find Utterly Useless. You *must* write a Nice Note anyway.

January 3, 2006

Dear Grandmother,

Thank you so much for the McDonald's gift certificates you sent! I have to stay away from the Big Macs myself (the doctor just told me to watch my cholesterol), but I'm certainly going to put them toward salads and Chicken McNuggets for lunch! I also sometimes take my Little Neighbor, Sally, for a Happy Meal, so we can use them then, too.

I hope you are well. How has the arthritis been lately? I hope you've been able to get out to the Bridge Club. Thanks again for thinking of me, Grams, and I'll call you soon.

Love,
Elizabeth

The Thank-You Note for Money

You must never, *ever* mention the amount of money than was given to you, regardless if it was five dollars or five million dollars, Dear Reader! To do so is Most Crass, and you will only sound as if you are Ungrateful, no matter what you say. We recommend Being Vague.

May 27, 2005

Dear Aunt Josephine and Uncle Erasmus,

Thank you so much for remembering me on my graduation from college! I've already deposited the check you sent in my Fund to Go To France and Study Art—I think I'll be able to go by next summer!

How is everything in Peoria? Has Lulu decided where she's going to college yet? You know I'm pushing for my alma mater, but then, I guess I'm a bit biased!

Thank you again for being so generous—I hope to get out for a wee visit sometime soon.

Love to all,
Josie

The Thank-You Note for The Thing-That-You-Can't-Identify

As with Unwanted Gifts, you will, at some point, probably receive something, and you won't know What the Heck It Is. We recommend that when writing your thank-you note that you Try Your Best; be vague, yet grateful.

November 2, 2007

Dear Arlene,

Thank you so much for your very generous wedding gift. Tom and I simply adore it, and, of course, have given it pride-of-place. You never waver in your thoughtfulness!

Thanks again, and I'm sure I'll be talking with you soon.

As ever,
Charlotte

The Second (Follow-Up) Thank-You Note

If someone gives you something, such as theatre tickets, a Trip Around the World, etc., you must write *two* thank-you notes. One upon receipt of the gift, and a second after you have used it, with some kind words about how much you enjoyed the play/trip/etc.

December 12, 2004

Dear Uncle Robert,

I just wanted to drop you a quick note and let you know how much I enjoyed "Long Day's Journey Into Night." I didn't have any problem picking up the tickets you so kindly told the box office to put aside for me, and it turned out the seats were terrific! I brought my friend Lily (you know how we both love O'Neill after being in "Ah, Wilderness!" together in High School!), and she was simply in seventh heaven, and sends her thanks along, too.

Thanks again—you're absolutely the best Uncle a girl could ask for!

Love Always,
Essie

The Bread-and-Butter Letter

After you have visited someone's house, especially overnight, you must write a thank-you note, and this particular form of The Thank-You Note is known as "The Bread-and-Butter Letter." Here's An Example.

March 14, 2006

Dear Mr. and Mrs. Whitney,

Thank you so much for putting me up when I was up looking at Cornell. Not only did you go above and beyond, but I don't remember when I last had so much fun—I think that was the most cutthroat game of Trivial Pursuit I've ever played . . . I'm still reeling! I also, of course, loved hearing all the stories about when you were in college with Mom, and looking at the photo albums. Thanks also for the driving tour of Ithaca. It really was too nice of you, especially since it was so snowy and dangerous out . . . I don't know how you natives manage to drive in all that freezing rain all winter!

Thanks again for such a grand time. Mom and Dad send their love, and we hope to come up for a visit this summer. I'll let you know as soon as I hear from Cornell!

Love,
Elsie

The Bread-and-Butter Letter for When You Had a *Really Terrible* Time

Even when you had the most God-awful time when visiting someone (e.g., you came down with Food Poisoning, the Dog Bit You, you sprained your ankle on the Mountain Hike you were forced to go upon), you *still* must Send Your Thanks. *ALWAYS*. And sound sincere about it, no less.

November 27, 2005

Dear Mr. and Mrs. Kensington-Smythe,

Thank you so much for having me to visit you and Cecily in New York this past weekend. My, such an exciting time! I feel like I had the "Full New York Experience"—it was good for me to get lost on the subway and get mugged! (Since it all turned out okay—I now have A Story to tell people!) More importantly, I loved meeting you and the rest of the family—I've heard so many good things about everybody from Cecily at school, and it was awfully good of you to take me in over the holiday, since I couldn't go home.

Thanks again for everything, and please give Rover a big, fuzzy hug for me!

Fondly,
Gertrude

The Condolence Letter

Nothing is more difficult than writing A Condolence Note, Dear Reader. Try to avoid trite phrases like, "Really, Bob's better off now," or "Bob's in a Better Place." Regardless of whether or not these things are true, they are overused expressions, and no, they will *not* comfort The Bereaved, who, we're sure, feel that Bob would be better off and/or in a better place if he were watching *Six Feet Under* in the Family Room than *actually* being Six Feet Under.

April 14, 2006

Dear Louisa,

    I was so saddened to hear of the sudden death of Elmer—the news came as such a shock to us all, and we'll all miss him terribly. I know that no one will ever play such a mean game of checkers as he!

    Please let me know if I can do anything at all for you at this terrible time. I'm always thinking of you, and my prayers are with you and your family.

Love,
Suzy

The Condolence Note for a Young Person/ Baby/Miscarriage

The Condolence Note is even more difficult to write if you're offering Your Sympathies for the death of a Young Person or Baby (and, yes, a miscarriage counts as a death), but you should not let this keep you from writing to The Family right away.

March 3, 2005

Dear Helen,

    James and I were shocked when we heard of Mimi's terrible accident. We can't even begin to imagine what you and William must be going through, not to mention the other kids. There are no words to express our sorrow.

Please let us know if we can help in any way, or give me a ring anytime you'd like to talk. Our prayers are with you all.

Love,
Bridget

The Formal Regret to an Invitation

The Formal Regret, with the exception of being handwritten, should follow the wording and spacing of the Invitation exactly. For example:

Mr. Patrick John Parker
regrets that he will be unable to accept
Mr. and Mrs. William Huntington Graves'
kind invitation for
Saturday, the third of June

The Informal Response to an Invitation

June 23, 2006

Dear Cynthia,

I'm so sorry that Amory and I will be unable to attend the luncheon you're having at your mother's house following your marriage ceremony at City Hall, as we'll be out of town that weekend, visiting Grandmother in Little Compton for her Annual Croquet Match. I'm so disappointed that we can't be there, as I'm sure it'll be lovely, and of course, we would love to be there to celebrate with you.

Best wishes to you and Henry, always.

Love,
Francie

"Going AWOL" (The P.P.C. Card)

As you know, Dear Reader, the EGs don't much care for Our Dear Friends Going AWOL, but if one must go On Sabbatical, it is proper to send your Calling Card to your Dear Friends and Acquaintances, on which you've written "pour prendre congé" (which is French for "to take [one's] leave") in ink in the lower left corner. Now, all your Dear Friends will not fret and fret about Your Sudden Absence from Their Social Circle, Your Disconnected 'Phone, and the Pile of Mail on Your Doorstep, because they will know that you're Not Dead, merely AWOL. Your Card should look like this:

Miss Emily Darlington Hunter

P. P. C.

If you *must* Go AWOL on the Spur of the Moment, then the EGs suggest you fill out our "AWOL Questionnaire," which you will find on pages 182–184, and distribute copies of it to Your Friends.

Dear John/Jane

It is, of course, always best to Break Up In Person, but sometimes (as in case of A Long War, for example) this is not feasible. However, Dear Reader, we urge you to sit down and write a nice letter rather than sending an e-mail or fax. Or worse, An Invitation to Your Wedding (to Someone Else).

January 22, 2007

Dear Abelard,

It is incredibly difficult to break this news to you, especially via letter, but as you've been away on your research project in the

Antarctic for the past five years without e-mail or telephone communication, I'm afraid this is the only way. I don't quite know how to say this, Dear Abelard, but things have a funny way of happening, and last week, Homer—you know—Homer Worthington from down the street—asked me to marry him. Homer and I have been spending a lot of time together lately, and, well, I said yes. I'm sorry, Dear Abelard, but I just can't sit on my hands waiting for you to come back from your Penguin Research. After all, you've given me no indication when you intend to return, and well, Abelard, I'm not getting any younger, you know. And now that Mom and Pops have both died, I'm free to leave the farm, so Homer and I are off to California, so he can pursue his screenwriting career, and I can work on my acting.

I'm sorry, Abelard. I can't expect you to want to stay friends, but I hope that everything will be all right by the time you return.

As ever,
Eloise

Business Letters

Business Letters differ from Personal Letters in Many Ways. We've included some examples of Business Letters You Might Want to Write below, but here are some simple guidelines before you begin:

- All letters must be printed by computer (or typed) in a clear, easy-to-read, normal font. (No **Comic Sans**, please!)

- All letters must be written on good-quality, buff or white 8½-by-11-inch paper.

- In the Upper-Right-Hand Corner, put your address (but not your name), and the date.

- Skip three lines, then aligned with the left margin, put "the inside address"—the name and address of the person to whom you are sending Your Letter.

- Skip three more spaces, then add your greeting: "Dear Mr. Smith:" A colon is More Formal than a comma.

- The body of your message should be clear, concise, and free from Spelling and Grammatical Errors.

- Your signature may be aligned with either the left-hand margin or your return address. Despite what Your Teacher told you in Fourth Grade, you may not close Business Letters with "Your friend." Good closings include, "Sincerely," "Yours truly," etc.

- Skip three lines, and print out Your Full Name. Sign your name in real blue or black ink above this.

A LETTER TO THE MANAGEMENT (PRAISE)

317 Greenfield Street
Hummelville, Illinois 67432
April 13, 2004

Mr. John President
Bigg's Department Store
423 Main Avenue
Milwaukee, Wisconsin 68752

Dear Mr. President:
I am writing concerning the marvelous staff you have in your China and Crystal Department. I walked into the store not knowing what on earth would go nicely with the china I recently inherited from my Grandmother, but your salesgirls, especially Anne Shirley, were incredibly helpful and patient with me as I selected crystal and linens. It is rare in this day and age to find this sort of service anywhere, especially in a large corporation like Bigg's Department Store. Please let your

staff know how much I appreciate their wisdom, kindness, patience, knowledge, and wit. Shopping at Bigg's is always a true joy.

Yours sincerely,

Mrs. James Windham

Mrs. James Windham

A LETTER TO THE MANAGEMENT (CRITICISM)

                          3940 Elm Boulevard
                          Apartment 607
                          Pittsburgh, Pennsylvania 15232
                          May 9, 2004

President
Yellow Taxi Company
421 Main Street
Pittsburgh, Pennsylvania 15200

Dear Sir or Madam:

I am writing to you to register my outrage over the way that one of your drivers treated me last Wednesday. Not only did the driver (it was car number 154, at approximately 10:30 A.M., Wednesday, May 4th) accuse me of being a liar (he said I had ordered a taxi to go to the airport, when in fact, I had ordered a taxi to go to City Hall), he was so surly that I feared for my life, especially when he took what he called "a necessary detour" through The Projects. Further, although I am not certain, I think that he was Intoxicated, as the taxi-cab smelled like A Brewery, and his driving was quite erratic. At the end of the ride, when I refused to tip the driver, due to the unsatisfactory service, he called me several names, which I shall not repeat, and attempted to hit me.

I am shocked and saddened, and for all my life Yellow Taxi Company has always been a trustworthy service, with the best of drivers. Rest assured that not only shall I never set foot in one of your taxi-cabs again, but I will also be registering a complaint with The Proper Authorities.

Yours sincerely,

Elizabeth Q. Grant

Elizabeth Q. Grant

A LETTER OF INQUIRY (FOR A JOB; COLD, OR FROM AN ADVERTISEMENT)

327 College Street
Apartment 6B
River City, Iowa 75542
June 21, 2004

Department of Human Resources
River City Museum of Art
1542 Main Street
River City, Iowa 75542

Dear Sir or Madam:

I am responding to your advertisement for a secretarial job that appeared in this Sunday's *Daily News*. As a lifelong patron of the arts, I am most anxious to begin my career in the administrative arts. As you can see from the enclosed résumé, I graduated this past spring from the University of Montana with a B.A. in Art History, and have spent the past four summers interning in the Docent Office at the Smithfield Art Museum, in my hometown of Small City, Minnesota.

Thank you for your consideration, and I look forward to hearing from you.

Sincerely yours,

Elizabeth Jane Montrose

Elizabeth Jane Montrose

For a cold (unsolicited) letter, you could merely substitute the first line with something like, "I am writing to you in hopes that there may be an entry-level position open at the River City Museum of Art." Whenever possible, try to find An Actual Person to whom you could address your letter. (For instance, the curator of the department in which you would like to work.)

A LETTER OF INTRODUCTION

Back in the Day, when you wanted to help An Acquaintance gain entry into a Social Circle, or recommend them for a job, you would give them a Letter of Introduction, which they would hand over to Your Important Friend, in lieu of a Personal Introduction from You. Nowadays, of course, most people just pick up the telephone or send off an e-mail, and say, "Hey, Millie, my kid Jimmy is moving to New York; would you take him under your wing?" However, every once in a while, a Real Letter (albeit a more informal one than in times past) is called for. Below, we offer An Example.

July 19, 2005

Dear Sarah,

My young nephew, Nigel, will be over in Germany this semester doing research for his Master's thesis on Silent Comedic German Film. He's found a flat over near the University, but I gave him your phone number in case of emergencies—I hope that's all right with you and Fritz. His mother (my older sister, Helen) and I'd appreciate it a great deal if you'd keep an unobtrusive eye on him while he's over there. His Poor Dear Mother is worried to death!

Thanks, and love to all,
Dottie

A LETTER TO AN ALUMNA/US OF YOUR SCHOOL (NETWORKING)
One of the great Advantages of having attended a Small Prep School or College is the "networking" benefits they offer. There are only so many Smallville College Graduates, as opposed to the millions of alumni of, say, The University of California. Thus, when one is fresh out of school, Alumni are a wonderful group to turn to for advice, and, one hopes, An Actual Job. (Although one can never come out and ask Mr. Big Alum for a Job, you can Flatter His Ego and ask for advice, which he will probably graciously hand out. You will then have A Mentor in Mr. Big Alum, and if you Hit It Off, you may well be offered a nice little internship in The Big Alum Company.)

307 Franklin Street
Apartment 507
Madison, Wisconsin 57329

Mr. John Smith
President
Big Alum Preservation, Inc.
Madison, Wisconsin 57021

Dear Mr. Smith,
I am a 1997 graduate of Dunston Prep (and a 2001 graduate of Smithfield College, in Parkville, Iowa; I also have my Master's in Architectural History from the University of Virginia), and I noticed in my Dunston Alumni Directory that you are an Architectural Preservationist here in Madison. I've been working to begin a career in Architectural

Preservation, and I was hoping that perhaps, as a seasoned veteran, you might have some helpful pointers for a bumbling novice such as myself.

I apologize for the intrusion; I know that I'm asking a lot, but any advice that you could possibly offer me would be most gratefully accepted.

Yours truly,

Reginald Mortimer Waltham

Reginald Mortimer Waltham, Dunston, '97

A LETTER OF RESIGNATION

As mentioned in Our First Book*, the Most Important thing about Quitting Your Job is that no matter how you feel, no matter *how* incompetent Your Boss is, you must never, ever Burn Your Bridges. You never know who knows whom, and who you'll meet again on your way up (or down) The Corporate Ladder. As gratifying as it may be to write, "You incompetent nincompoops, my cat would be better at running this damn place than you! I've had it up to *here*, and I quit, *quit, QUIT!!!!!!* Thanks for playing, you idiots! *PBBBTTTT!!!*", it's really better to stick to the form below. Even if you don't have another job lined up before you quit, it's best to Be Vague, rather than letting on you'd rather be homeless than spend another day in Your Cubicle.

347 Treeless Avenue
Brooklyn, New York 10234
May 1, 2005

Ms. Pamela Flannery
Horrible, Horrible & Worse
4932 Fifth Avenue
New York, New York 10020

Dear Ms. Flannery,
I regret that as of Friday, May 24th, I must resign from my position at Horrible, Horrible & Worse for personal reasons. I have learned

much during my three years working for you, and regret that I must now depart.

Sincerely yours,

Anne W. Gardiner

Anne W. Gardiner

*For Further Information, please refer to our First Book, *Things You Need to be Told*, The Berkley Publishing Group, a division of Penguin Group (USA) Inc., 2001. Thank you so much.

Questions and Answers on Various and Sundry

Dear Etiquette Grrls,

Is it really necessary to send thank-you notes for wedding gifts? Wouldn't a mass e-mail do just as well?

Yours in Earnest,
Too Busy

Dear Too Busy,

1) *YES!!!!!!!* 2) *ABSOLUTELY NOT!!!!*

Yours in Shock and Horror,
The Etiquette Grrls

P.S. You might want to refer to pages 1–215 [last pg] in This Volume as well as pages 1–204 in *Things You Need to Be Told* before you ask the Etiquette Grrls any other Questions, Dear Reader.

Dear Etiquette Grrls,

I am such a procrastinator!!!!! I am a terrible, horrible person!!!!! I shall Burn in the Fires of Hell For All Eternity!!! You shall never, ever

*find it in your hearts to forgive me, dearest Etiquette Grrls!!!!! You see, I
declined an invitation to a wedding which occurred two weeks ago and
I have not yet sent a gift. I am really, really embarrassed about this and
I just don't know what to do . . . I bought the gift (a lovely silver Paul
Revere bowl) some time ago, and it's sitting right here in the bag, but I
just don't know what I should say . . . won't my friends the Bride and
Groom think I'm frightfully lazy? Especially as I didn't go to the wedding,
either? (I feel terrible about that, too, but I had a Prior Engagement, and
it was all the way across the country, and I simply couldn't make it.)
But golly, I wouldn't be surprised if they never speak to me again.*

Yours faithfully,
Guilt-Stricken, Sobbing

Dear Guilt-Stricken, Sobbing,

   Good heavens, Dear Reader! Stop Beating Yourself Up! The Etiquette Grrls aren't going to Have You Shot, or anything! The
Etiquette Grrls have never seen any of their Dear Readers more
overwhelmed with guilt than you, Dear Reader! Are you Catholic,
perchance? Just wondering. (The Etiquette Grrls are, and we know
all about That Guilt Thing.) But anyway . . . pull yourself together
and listen to the Etiquette Grrls. You have done nothing Terrible,
Dear Reader . . . It's not like you said "Dear Etiquette Grrls, I didn't
attend My Only Brother's Wedding, and the gift I bought for him
and my new sister-in-law has been sitting on my coffee table for
the past four years, and I'm just Too Lazy to go to the P.O. It's
an espresso maker; I think at this point I might just keep it and
use it myself. Is that okay, Dear Etiquette Grrls?" (That's not the
case here, is it, Dear Reader? Tell the Etiquette Grrls the truth,
now!) True, the Etiquette Grrls are Sticklers for Promptness, but a
two-week delay in getting a wedding gift in the post is not a Big
Deal in the Grand Scheme of Things, even in the Etiquette Grrls'
eyes. After all, Your Friends are probably not even back from their
Honeymoon! Just wrap up The Gift in pretty paper, pack it well

in a sturdy box for shipping, and enclose a wee note saying that you're so sorry you couldn't attend The Wedding, but your thoughts were with Your Friends, and that you wish them much happiness, blah, blah, blah. (There's no need to mention Your Guilt over not sending The Gift more promptly.) And then take it down to the Post Office and send it on its Merry Way! It's that easy, Dear Reader! And stop being so Hard on Yourself!

Yours truly,
The Etiquette Grrls

Dear Etiquette Grrls,

I was married recently, and I never received a wedding gift from my Maid of Honor. Now, I know of course, gifts are always entirely optional, but, well, my Maid of Honor is a Very Dear Lifelong Friend, and it just seems a little odd that she wouldn't have sent anything. She is, after all, a Very Generous Girl. This makes me wonder if perhaps there was some sort of SNAFU and maybe her gift somehow was misplaced. My husband and I are both terribly keen on writing thank-you notes, and it's been bothering us both to think that somebody might think we are remiss in doing so. What should we do, do you think? Thank you, Dear Etiquette Grrls.

Married in Michigan

Dear Married,

Well, have you spoken to your Maid of Honor lately, Dear Reader? Has she been unusually Cold and Distant? If so, then, yes, we think it's probably likely that she did, in fact, send you A Fabulous Gift, and she is un peu peeved that you didn't send a thank-you note. If not, however, the Etiquette Grrls can think of Three Possible Scenarios:

(1) She didn't send you a gift. (Which the Etiquette Grrls agree with you, Dear Reader, would be a wee bit peculiar.)

(2) She did send you a gift, but she is not a Thank-You Note Writer herself, and thus, doesn't care that you failed to send her one.

(3) She is un peu forgetful, and it has slipped her mind that she sent you a gift, or that you failed to send a thank-you note.

If you suspect that the gift has, in fact, gone AWOL, Dear Reader, the first thing you might do is to inquire around to the other Members of the Wedding, and see if maybe anyone remembers your MOH mentioning it. Who knows; she might very well have told them all about the great retro cocktail shaker she found for you. If, however, this Line of Questioning proves Unfruitful, you might try dropping your MOH a wee note. You might say something along the lines of the following:

Dear Bitsy,

I just wanted to thank you for being my Maid of Honor at my wedding last month. William and I couldn't have been happier that you were a member of the wedding party. You know it just wouldn't have been the same without you, Bitsy, dear.

William and I have found ourselves in just a bit of an embarrassing situation, though—we're both just Beside Ourselves. William's brother John, who as you remember was Best Man, mentioned to us that he thought he remembered you telling him that you had sent us a silver cocktail shaker. I'm afraid that if you did (and it's perfectly all right if you didn't, as your presence at the wedding is the best gift we could have asked for), it must have been misplaced or lost in the post. I only mention it in case you thought we were snubbing you by not promptly sending a thank-you note (you know how William and I are both Very Prompt Letter-Writers), and also, we fear that perhaps Something Terrible might have happened, and you were charged by the store for something which never arrived at its destination. Do let us know what the story is, Bitsy, dear, so William and I can stop fretting . . . you know what a Worrywart Bill is, the Silly Old Thing!

Again, we're so pleased that you were able to be in our wedding. It truly meant a lot to me that you were my Maid of Honor. I hope that all is well with you in San Francisco, and that we can get together soon!

Love,
Kitty

When phrased like this, there's no implication that you're Fishing For Presents—you're just looking after Bitsy's Best Interests. After all, she'll surely appreciate knowing if she should ring up Crate & Barrel and give them A Stern Talking-To.

Yours truly,
The Etiquette Grrls

Dear Etiquette Grrls,

I must beg your pardon. I have committed an unforgivable faux pas. A benefactor had given me a considerable amount in funds to help me go on The Grand Tour. My mother told me to write a thank-you letter before I left on my travels, but I insisted that I wait until after I returned, so I could tell my benefactor what I did and saw, as I knew he would enjoy hearing about my adventures. However, when I got back from my trip, Mama announced that my benefactor had Met With An Untimely Demise. I feel I must still send a thank-you note, but to whom I'm not sure. My Kind Benefactor was a widower, so should I send something to his daughter?

I await your reply with great angst.

Sincerely,
Naughty Young Man

Dear Naughty Young Man,

Well, well, well. While the Etiquette Grrls offer our Most Sincere Sympathies to you, Dear Reader, we feel we shall have to make you Our Official Poster Boy for Why You Should Write Thank-You Notes Promptly. Not to be Too Morbid, but next time you decide to postpone writing that Thank-You Note to your Great Aunt Agnes in favor of a Quick Trip to Bendel's, remember: While you're pawing through the cashmere sweaters, She Might Keel Over Dead. You just never know, Dear Reader.

Regarding whether or not you should delay writing a thank-you note for a gift until after you've enjoyed it (applicable to many kinds of gifts, including travel, theatre tickets, etc.), we think it is always best to write two notes: once immediately after receiving the gift, and again after one has enjoyed it.

However, we are not trying to Beat You Up over this, Dear Reader. What's done is done, and we commend you for trying to do the Right Thing now. Yes, absolutely, you should write to your benefactor's daughter. This should be more of a sympathy note than a thank-you note directed at an Alternate Person, however. We think you should say something like, "I was so sorry to hear of your father's unexpected death. I will always remember his great kindness and generosity . . .", and tell her a little bit about how much his gift meant to you and what it allowed you to experience. We're sure she will be pleased to hear about how much you appreciated her Poor Dear Father's generosity.

Very truly yours,
The Etiquette Grrls

CHAPTER FOUR

That's Entertainment!

Perhaps, Dear Reader, you think that all you need to know in life is to say, "Please," and "Thank you," and how to Play Well with Others. Well, yes, of course that's a Good Start, but the well-mannered, well-educated, well-rounded, Interesting Person is able to carry on An Interesting, Engaging Conversation with everyone from the Deli Clerk to the President of the United States. We happen to think that The Arts are always A Good Topic of Conversation, as is any sort of Pop Culture, such as Television, or Movies, or even, dare we say it, Sports. The Point, Dear Reader, is that you should take It Upon Yourself to Know a Bit About Everything. The Etiquette Grrls have yet to open the Doors of The Etiquette Grrls' Academy of Politesse and Common Knowledge, but you can begin Your Education by heading to the library and/or the video store, and checking out as many of the following books and films and recordings as possible. We've also included a few words on The Necessity of Knowing How to Dance Without Looking Like You're Flailing Around Like A Dying Halibut, and lest you think the EGs aren't any fun at all, a bit about popular pastimes like watching television and sports.

Hooray for Hollywood!: The Films You Need to Watch (Or at Least a Rudimentary List Thereof)

Forget all of the AFI's Assorted Lists of Top 100 Movies of All Time. Forget those drippy "Cinematherapy" girls. We, the Etiquette Grrls, have made a List of Movies You Need to See. We do not claim that all of the movies on this list are Groundbreaking, Seminal Movies, nor that they are all The Greatest Movies of All Time. One or two of them aren't even very good. Nor, unfortunately, are we able to list *all* the movies we love and that you absolutely need to see, in the interest of space. (Maybe one day someone will ask us to write *Things You Need to Be Told About the History of Cinema*—our well-manicured fingers are crossed!) Nor is this list intended to provide you with a synopsis of these films, à la Leonard Maltin. You, Dear Reader, will have to watch them all yourself to discover Why These Are Our Favorite Movies. But what they are, are Films You Must See Before You Die. Yes, lots of them are Black and White. (Why do people mind that? We don't get that *AT ALL*!! Black and White Film is a *BEAUTIFUL, STUNNING MEDIUM*!!!!) Yes, lots of them are old. (*AGAIN*, what do people have against Old Movies?!) Yes, there will be A Test. (We want to make sure you learn this stuff! It's For Your own Good, Dear Reader! We don't want to hear any complaints about it!)

12 Angry Men—1957. Henry Fonda, Jack Klugman, and Ensemble Cast. Directed by Sidney Lumet. Perhaps the Best Courtroom Drama Ever. Well, make that The Best Jury-Room Movie of All Time. Skip the recent TV Remake. Brilliant cinematography. Note that none of the characters have names during the *vast* majority of the film.

To Kill a Mockingbird—1962. Gregory Peck, Robert Duvall. Directed by Robert Mulligan. The Other Best Courtroom Drama of All Time. Based on Harper Lee's wonderful, wonderful novel. Duvall's first-ever movie!

Anatomy of a Murder—1959. James Stewart, Lee Remick. Directed by Otto Preminger. The Other-Other Best Courtroom Drama of All Time.

Picnic—1955. William Holden, Kim Novak, Rosalind Russell. Directed by Joshua Logan. A Good, Character-Driven film with a strong ensemble cast. About a good-hearted drifter, and what happens when he drifts into Smalltown, U.S.A. Based on William Inge's play. Note that a young Susan Strasberg (daughter of Lee Strasberg, founder of The Actor's Studio; also Marilyn's pal—and if you don't know who we mean by "Marilyn," you've clearly been living under a rock, and need to enroll in American Icons 101 before the Etiquette Grrls can even begin to guide you through the fascinating medium of film) plays Kim's Little Sis.

Cape Fear—1962. Gregory Peck, and Robert Mitchum, being the Rottenest Guy You Ever Saw. Directed by J. Lee Thompson. The De Niro remake's got *nothing*, and the Etiquette Grrls mean *nothING* on this one!

Night of the Hunter—1955. Shelley Winters, Lillian Gish (yes, the one from the silent movies), and Mitchum again, scaring the livin' bejesus out of you. (Note to self: Never trust Itinerant "Ministers" with anything tattooed on their knuckles.) Directed by Charles Laughton (the actor, husband of Elsa Lanchester).

Elmer Gantry—1960. Burt Lancaster, Jean Simmons, Shirley Jones (yes, of *The Partridge Family* fame, playing a prostitute!). Directed by Richard Brooks. This time, the Itinerant, Bible-Thumping Minister's a Good Guy. (A bit of a Con, but a Good Guy nonetheless.) Based on Sinclair Lewis' novel, and you know how the Etiquette Grrls feel about American Literature Between the Wars.

To Sir, With Love—1967. Sidney Poitier. Directed by James Clavell. A gentle, novice teacher comes to a Terrible, Poor, Inner-City School in Swingin' Mod London. There's even A Montage of Mod London. Need we say more? Okay, we will. Lulu. *And* viewers of PBS will recognize *Keeping Up Appearances'* and *Hetty Wainthrope Investigates'* Patricia Routledge as a fellow schoolteacher.

The Blackboard Jungle—1955. Anne Francis, Louis Calhern, and Glenn Ford as the beleaguered teacher this time. Directed by Richard Brooks. Much like the above, only in the '50s, and in inner-city New York. Darn that Rock and Roll! Look for a Very Young Klinger (Jamie Farr from *M*A*S*H*), using his Real Name (Jameel Farah) as one of the hoodlums. Also features a Young Sidney Poitier. (V. Ironic, see above.)

Rear Window—1954. Stewart. Kelly. Hitchcock. Enough said, really. Oh, and the guy across the courtyard? That's a chubby and white-haired Raymond Burr, of *Perry Mason* fame. Girls, study Kelly's clothes carefully, and copy them exactly!

The Trouble with Harry—1955. Shirley Maclaine (in her debut screen role), John Forsythe, and Jerry Mathers (of *Leave It to Beaver* fame). Directed by Alfred Hitchcock. Hitch does comedy? Yep. And well, too!

Psycho—1960. Anthony Perkins, Janet Leigh. Need we say anything about this one, really? It's actually sort of over-rated, but you simply *have* to see it. Several Times. And directed by Hitchcock, of course. But of course you knew that already, Dear Reader—the Etiquette Grrls really needn't have even said.

Strangers on a Train—1951. Robert Walker, Farley Granger. Another great Hitchcock film, based on a novel by Patricia Highsmith, of *The Talented Mr. Ripley* (1999), which, actually, was a pretty good film, too, despite Matt and Gwyneth. Backs up what Your Mother Told You about Never Talking to Strangers.

Shadow of a Doubt—1943. Teresa Wright, Joseph Cotton. Screenplay by Thornton Wilder! And, oh yeah, directed by Good Ol' A. H. Oh, hell, just go out and see *EVERYTHING* directed by Hitch. Except for his last two completed Feature Films, *Frenzy* and *Family Plot*, both of which Stink.

To Have and Have Not—1944. Bogie. Bacall. This is the one that made them a team, kiddos. Also contains the line, "You know how to whistle, don't you? You just put your lips together and blow." And, oh yeah, based on a Hemingway story. Directed by the brilliant Howard Hawks, who could Do It All.

Breakfast at Tiffany's—1961. Audrey Hepburn, George Peppard. What the EGs watch whenever they're sad, lonely, and have a bad case of the "Mean Reds." Directed by Blake Edwards.

Thoroughly Modern Millie—1967. Julie Andrews, Mary Tyler Moore, Carol Channing, Beatrice Lilly, James Fox, John Gavin. Directed by George Roy Hill. Even though it was a Box-Office Flop, and panned by The Critics, we loved this movie long before anyone even *thought* of turning it into a hit Broadway Musical! Is it Un Peu Corny? Yes, it is, but it's *supposed* to be—it's *satire*, Dear Reader! Better than the Broadway stage version. (We're sorry, Sutton Foster may be talented, but she's no Julie Andrews. And the rest of the cast certainly can't compare to that of the film!)

Roman Holiday—1953. Audrey again, with Gregory Peck, on location in Rome. The film that made Hepburn A Star. Directed by William Wyler.

Sabrina—1954. Audrey yet again, with an aging Bogie and Bill Holden. Snappy dialogue, and worth it just for Audrey's clothes. (Givenchy, although the credits say Edith Head.) Would have been made better with the original casting of Cary Grant in Bogart's role. (Plus, rumor has it that Bogie was mean to Dear Audrey on the set! How could he! If only the EGs could give Mr. Bogart a Good, Stern Talking-To!) Again, the brilliant Billy Wilder directs and writes.

Singing in the Rain—1952. Gene Kelly, Debbie Reynolds, Donald O'Connor, Jean Hagen. Possibly The Best Musical Ever Made. Will have you whistling for *DAYS*, and you will go around imitating Hagen's *brilliant* "Innnd Eiiiii Caaaiiiin't Staaaaaind 'im!" for The Rest of Your Life! Directed by Stanley Donen and Mr. Kelly himself!

The Philadelphia Story—1940. Cary Grant, Kate Hepburn, James Stewart. Fabulous screwball comedy. One of the very best of the genre. Based on the stage play by the same name. Directed by George Cukor.

High Society—1956. Bing Crosby, Frank Sinatra, Grace Kelly, Celeste Holm. Exact same story as above, only with music, and set in Newport, Rhode Island, during the World-Famous Jazz Festival (which means some cameo appearances from Louis Armstrong!). Inebriated Bing and Frank do a great number in the Library during The Party Scene. Directed by Charles Waters. Watch this and the above film, and write a three-to-five-page compare and contrast essay for the Etiquette Grrls, please!

Mister Roberts—1955. Henry Fonda, Jack Lemmon, William Powell, James Cagney (and James Cagney's Palm Tree). Wonderful, marvelous story about a ship and its men during WWII. Not really a War Movie, more of a Character Study. You'll laugh! You'll cry! You'll want to punch Cagney in the nose! One of Fonda's very best movies. Directed by John Ford and Mervyn LeRoy.

Gentlemen Prefer Blondes—1953. Marilyn Monroe, Jane Russell. Howard Hawks' only musical. One great movie, with two Swell Dames. Contains the number "Diamonds Are a Girl's Best Friend," which Madonna ripped off for her "Material Girl" video. (Sacrilege! The Etiquette Grrls can hear Miss Monroe Spinning in Her Grave!) Based on Anita Loos' novel.

His Girl Friday—1940. Cary Grant, Rosalind Russell. Another Hawks-directed film, with some of the snappiest dialogue around. Based on the stage play, *The Front Page*, only Hawks made the character of "Hildy" a girl (Russell)—yay! Our favorite line? Russell to Grant, "Walter, you're wonderful, in a loathsome sort of way!" Second favorite line? Grant to Russell, re: Her Fiancé: "He looks like that actor, whatshisname, Ralph Bellamy." (It *is* Ralph Bellamy.)

Bringing Up Baby—1938. Cary Grant, Kate Hepburn. Another classic screwball from the '30s. Grant and Hepburn chase a runaway leopard all over town, singing "I Can't Give You Anything But Love, Baby." Implausible, but true. Again, directed by Howard Hawks. (Can you tell that we adore Mr. Hawks, Dear Reader?)

Mr. Blandings Builds His Dream House—1948. Grant, yet again, with Myrna Loy. Uproariously funny! Why you should never attempt to Build Your Own House. How comforting that one had Terrible Problems with contractors, and the like, even Back in the Day. Directed by H. C. Potter.

It Happened One Night—1934. Claudette Colbert, Clark Gable. Unfortunately, Gable lets gentlemen think that it's perfectly okay to not wear An Undershirt. (Which it is not; please see page 42.) The Etiquette Grrls adore Mr. Gable, but we would like to have a few words with him about that. (Un peu difficile, seeing as he's a little on the dead side, unfortunately. But the EGs will figure out something, fear not!) Colbert shows us (and Mr. Tough-Guy Gable) how to Hitchhike, which, obviously, we do *NOT* condone, but the world was a whole lot safer in 1934. Sigh. Directed by Frank Capra.

The Manchurian Candidate—1962. Frank Sinatra, Laurence Harvey, Angela Lansbury, Janet Leigh. Another fantastic ensemble cast, and a great performance from Sinatra. The film's release date was pushed back due to President Kennedy's Assassination. (As the film is about the assassination of a President, its original release date was Rawther Poor Timing, to say the least.) Directed by John Frankenheimer.

Some Like It Hot—1959. Tony Curtis, Jack Lemmon, Marilyn Monroe. Possibly the Best Comedy of All Time, directed by Billy Wilder. See Curtis and Lemmon in Drag! See Curtis and Lemmon in *Flapper* Drag!! Curtis' Cary Grant Impression is brilliant, as is Lemmon's retort, "No-bod-y Taa-lks like that!"

Network—1976. Faye Dunaway, Peter Finch, William Holden, Robert Duvall, and a Good Ensemble Cast. The film from which we get the phrase, *"I'M MAD AS HELL, AND I'M NOT GONNA TAKE IT ANYMORE!!!"* Directed by Sidney Lumet.

Casablanca—1942. Humphrey Bogart, Ingrid Bergman, numerous other Luminaries. More Famous Lines per minute than in any other movie. For the record, and contrary to popular belief, Bogie never says, "Play it again, Sam." What he *does* say is, "Play it, Sam. Play 'As Time Goes By.' " Sam, incidentally, is played by Dooley Wilson. We're Sick to Death of seeing misinformation about Who Played Sam in Trivia Games and the like! The Etiquette Grrls' Favorite Line: "Of all the Gin Joints in all of the world, she had to walk into mine." (You know how the EGs do like Their Gin, Dear Reader.) Directed by Michael Curtiz.

Whatever Happened to Baby Jane?—1962. An aging, crazy Bette Davis. An aging, crazy Joan Crawford. Pitted against each other. Need the EGs say any more? Directed by Robert Aldrich.

Mommie Dearest—1981. Faye Dunaway. "NO. WIRE. HANGERS. EVER!!!!!!" The Etiquette Grrls aren't at all keen on wire hangers, either (they're Bad For Your Clothes), but we're not quite so obsessive-compulsive about it, thank goodness. About the aforementioned Miss Crawford and her adopted children. And you thought that *you* had a Troubled Relationship avec Your Mother, Dear Reader! Renting this will be a heck of a lot cheaper than going to Your Shrink, and you'll feel much, much better afterward. Directed by Frank Perry.

All About Eve—1950. Bette Davis. *TRULY* Bette at her Best! "Fasten your *SEAT*-belts, it's Go-ing to be a *BUM*-py Night!" With Anne Baxter, Gary Merrill (Bette's husband—one of them, anyway), George Sanders, Celeste Holm. And if that weren't enough, Marilyn in one of her earliest roles! Directed by Joseph L. Mankiewicz.

√ *Gone With the Wind*—1939. Vivien Leigh, Clark Gable, Olivia DeHavilland, Leslie Howard. Love it or hate it, you gotta see it. Unabridged, with no commercials. Also many Famous Lines. FSF '17 was one of many (uncredited) writers who worked on the script. Directed by Victor Fleming (among others). MGM went through directors and writers like water on this one, Dear Reader. But it turned out okay in the end, no? Based on Margaret Mitchell's 1937 Pulitzer Prize–winning novel.

√ *The Wizard of Oz*—1939. Judy Garland, Ray Bolger, Jack Haley, Bert Lahr. Again, another movie that you can't say you've Lived until you've seen in its entirety. As far as the Etiquette Grrls know, all the rumors about Misbehavior, Death of Munchkins, etc., on-set are all Glaring Lies. And please don't bother the Etiquette Grrls (or anyone else) with any silly talk about how the film syncs with Pink Floyd's *Dark Side of the Moon*. The Etiquette Grrls could tell you about how the scene in *Mary Poppins* with the carousel horses running a race syncs perfectly with Cake's "The Distance," but frankly, we can't be bothered. Directed by Victor Fleming, and based on L. Frank Baum's novel. The Etiquette Grrls beg of you, *do not* see *any* of the sequels or remakes of this film, but *do* read the rest of Mr. Baum's series about Oz.

From Here to Eternity—1953. Burt Lancaster, Montgomery Clift, Deborah Kerr, Frank Sinatra, Donna Reed. Wonderful, wonderful, wonderful story set in Hawaii in the days leading up to the Attack on Pearl Harbor. Sinatra is marvelous in a Dramatic, Non-Singing Role. Directed by Fred Zinnemann.

A Place in the Sun—1951. Montgomery Clift, Elizabeth Taylor, Shelley Winters. Based on Dreiser's *An American Tragedy* (which you should definitely read, Dear Reader), which was based on a True Story. A bit of a downer, but well worth it. And dig Liz's Swell White Dress! Directed by George Stevens.

Laura—1944. Dana Andrews, Gene Tierney. One of the Etiquette Grrls' very Favorite Mystery Movies. (And, oh, how we *love* Dana Andrews!) Great supporting acting, too, from Clifton Webb, as gossip-hound Waldo Lydecker. Vincent Price is in this one, too, before he got Creepy! (Yes, Dear Reader! Before he was in hilariously bad Horror Flicks, and before he hosted PBS' *Mystery!*, Mr. Price used to be a Matinee Idol! It's true! Trust us!) We could watch this one a million times. Directed by Otto Preminger.

Rebecca—1940. Joan Fontaine, Laurence Olivier, George Sanders. Judith Anderson *is* Mrs. Danvers. <shiver!> One of the few films the EGs can think of, based on one of their favorite books (Daphne du Maurier's novel of the same name is An Annual Read for Us!)

that turned out fine. The best movie version of du Maurier's novel by far! Directed by Our Dear Friend, Alfred Hitchcock.

The Best Years of Our Lives—1946. Myrna Loy, Fredric March, Dana Andrews, Teresa Wright, Virginia Mayo. *SUPERB* Ensemble Cast! *THE BEST POSTWAR MOVIE EVER MADE!!!!* Take note in particular of Harold Russell, who was not an actor, but a Real-Life Vet, who really did lose both his hands in the war. He never made another movie, but he did win, in addition to winning that year's Academy Award for Best Actor in a Supporting Role, an Honorary Oscar, "For bringing hope and courage to his fellow veterans through his appearance in *The Best Years of Our Lives*." Not too shabby for a non-actor type. Directed by William Wyler.

Butch Cassidy and the Sundance Kid—1969. Paul Newman. Robert Redford. The Etiquette Grrls, generally speaking, aren't too big on Westerns. But come on. Redford. Newman. Need we say more? Directed by George Roy Hill. Have a double feature with *The Sting* (1973), also directed by Mr. Hill, wherein Redford and Newman play some Pretty Damn Cool Con Men in the 1930s.

Cool Hand Luke—1967. Paul Newman. As with Westerns, the Etiquette Grrls aren't Too Big on Jail Movies. But, boy, That Newman Guy is the keenest! Directed by Stuart Rosenberg.

Mr. Smith Goes to Washington—1939. Jimmy Stewart teaches us all about how politics *should* be. A film for us all to watch and learn from. Directed by Frank Capra, of course.

Heaven Knows, Mr. Allison—1957. An unlikely, but sweet story about a Marine, Robert Mitchum, stranded on a deserted Pacific Island with a Nun, Deborah Kerr, during the middle of World War II. Directed by John Huston. (And you think that *Survivor* is good,

Dear Reader? Are there ever any *NUNS* on *Survivor*, Dear Reader? The Etiquette Grrls think not.)

✓ *Dead Poets Society*—1989. Robin Williams, Robert Sean Leonard, Ethan Hawke, Josh Charles, Gale Hansen, etc. The movie that, if you are one of the Etiquette Grrls, our Boarding School Roommate, or our Boarding School Best Friend/Next-Door Neighbor, you know the dialogue of, and every *SINGLE* nuance of, by heart. In fact, if you are any of the above-listed people, you can *frighten* the actors who appeared in the film by your terrifyingly clear memory of the Dialogue and Blocking of Every Single Scene. One can also adapt bits of dialogue to Your Everyday Patois (and if you are the Etiquette Grrls and/or their Dear Friends, you already have done so . . . i.e., "If I were ever to buy a drink . . . twice . . . I would probably buy *this* one. *Both* times!").

✓ *Rushmore*—1998. Jason Schwartzman, Bill Murray. One of the very best Recent Movies. Another Private School movie, but very different from *DPS*. Directed by Wes Anderson.

✓ *Swing Kids*—1993. Robert Sean Leonard, Christian Bale, Frank Whaley. A Good Movie, which suffered from Bad Timing, as it was released a few years before the Swing Craze, and (we think), some Bad Editing that leaves a few Plot Holes. The mish-mash of accents is also un peu perplexing, especially British Christian Bale's American Accent, considering Fellow Brit Kenneth Branagh uses his native accent. But nevermind. Swell music, and swing dancing to your heart's content! Oh, and *ER*'s Noah Wylie plays a Nasty Little Nazi Bad Guy! Directed by Thomas Carter.

Auntie Mame—1958. The Fabulous Rosalind Russell, playing one of the Most Fabulous Women who Ever Lived. (Auntie Mame was Mame Dennis, a Real Person, and A Real Eccentric.) Includes a

Good Scene with a Good Example of the Infamous Locust Valley Lockjaw Accent. Directed by Morton DaCosta.

Much Ado About Nothing—1993. Kenneth Branagh, Emma Thompson, Robert Sean Leonard, Kate Beckinsale, Denzel Washington, Michael Keaton, Keanu Reeves. Directed by Mr. Branagh. Here's a concept! Shakespeare *without* Some Dumb Gimmick—and it's Perfectly Understandable and Enjoyable! It's even, dare we say it, *fun!* Set in the beautiful Tuscan countryside! Mr. Reeves, as our beloved Dorothy Parker once said of (our also beloved) Katharine Hepburn, "runs the gamut of emotions from 'A' to 'B,' " but that aside, it's a really keen, feel-good movie. (And educational, too!)

The Bachelor and the Bobby-Soxer—1947. Myrna Loy, Cary Grant, Shirley Temple (as a teen-ager!). Light, amusing film. Contrary to popular belief, the routine "You remind me of the man./What man?/The man with the power./What power?/Hoo-doo./Hoo-doo?/You do./Do what?/Remind me of the man," etc., is from this movie, not *Labyrinth* (1986). Well, actually, the Etiquette Grrls strongly suspect that it's An Old Vaudeville Routine, à la Abbot and Costello's "Who's on First?" but trust us, it is *not* from *Labyrinth*. We have actually Come to Blows with people over this. As if anyone would be so silly to question the EGs' knowledge of Pop Culture! Directed by Irving Reis.

How to Marry a Millionaire—1953. Impoverished Department Store Models Lauren Bacall, Betty Grable, and Marilyn Monroe are Out on the Prowl. Marilyn at her Comedic Best. Directed by Jean Negulesco.

✓ *Pulp Fiction*—1994. A strong ensemble cast, including John Travolta, Samuel L. Jackson, and Uma Thurman. Directed by Quentin Tarantino, of course. A contemporary favorite of the Etiquette Grrls'. We could go on and on defending the film against all the critics who said it was nothing but Gratuitous Violence, but we shall refrain from doing so. We'll just say One Thing: *irony*, Dear Reader, *i-ron-y*. Also, the *keenest* Soundtrack, and many good quotable lines.

Reservoir Dogs—1992. Tarantino again, bringing together yet another ensemble cast, including Harvey Keitel, Tim Roth, and Steve Buscemi. Grittier, and more low-budget than *Pulp Fiction*, but we respect that. You'll never be able to hear "Stuck in the Middle with You" again without cringing.

✓ *Fight Club*—1999. Brad Pitt, Edward Norton, Helena Bonham Carter. Another contemporary film which caught unwarranted criticism for its violence (which is not gratuitous). Why is this on Our List? The Etiquette Grrls know this because Tyler Durden knows this. We also like it because EGH (loooooong before the movie) had the chenille bathrobe Brad Pitt wears in the movie. Watch for lots of Inside Jokes, like a bus passing, advertising Pitt's *Seven Years in Tibet*. Directed by David Fincher.

The African Queen—1951. An Aging, Cranky Kate Hepburn matches wits on a leaky old boat with An Aging, Cranky Humphrey Bogart, who does love His Gin. Shot on location. (And again, we say, "You think *Survivor* is good? Do you think *ANY* of those Twits on that show would last a *SECOND* against Hepburn or Bogart?") Directed by John Huston.

Metropolitan—1990. Chris Eigeman and Ensemble Cast. Directed by Whit Stillman. If the Etiquette Grrls were in their Late Teens in the early 1980s, and lived in New York City, our lives probably would have been much like this. Be prepared for a lot of talking and very little action, as with all of Stillman's brilliant films.

Pillow Talk—1959. Doris Day, Rock Hudson, Tony Randall. Cute. Directed by Michael Gordon.

That Touch of Mink—1962. Doris Day, Cary Grant, Gig Young. Cute. Directed by Delbert Mann.

Fargo—1996. William H. Macy, Frances McDormand, Steve Buscemi. Another of those post-post-modern cleverly ironic black comedies that the EGs are so fond of. Directed by Joel Coen.

Arsenic and Old Lace—1944. Cary Grant. One of *the* Best Screwball Comedies *ever*. Based on the stage play. Directed by Frank Capra. Please, please, *please*, will someone cast the Etiquette Grrls in a production of this? We've been begging and pleading since seventh grade!!!

The Big Sleep—1946. Humphrey Bogart, Lauren Bacall. Ooooh, do we *adore* Film Noir! Based on Raymond Chandler's terrifically good novel. Why can't our lives be like a Film Noir Movie? In Black and White, and the Whole Nine? Directed by Howard Hawks, and screenplay by Our Beloved Mr. William Faulkner.

The Postman Always Rings Twice—1946. Lana Turner, John Garfield. More Film Noir!! Jeepers, we could watch this stuff all day! Based on James M. Cain's novel. Directed by Tay Garnett.

Double Indemnity—1944. Barbara Stanwyck, Fred MacMurray. See Above. Directed by Billy Wilder. Can you tell that the EGs just can't get enough Film Noir?

Bell, Book, and Candle—1958. Kim Novak, Jack Lemmon, James Stewart. A Good Witch, A Wacky Warlock, and Poor Hapless Stewart mix it up in San Francisco. Another Entirely Overlooked Movie. Directed by Richard Quine.

√ *The Muppet Movie*—1979. Kermit the Frog, Miss Piggy, Fozzie Bear, The Other Muppets, assorted Cameo Appearances by People Who

Were Famous in 1979. Directed by James Frawley. How could anyone *not* like this movie? Better than all its sequels. The Very First Movie the Etiquette Grrls saw in a Movie Theatre. We own the soundtrack on LP, which we still listen to on the keen portable record player we had when we were about Four.

Lilies of the Field—1963. Sidney Poitier. The wonderful Mr. Poitier helps some Nuns build their much-needed chapel. (Have you noticed, dear Reader, that the EGs like Movies avec Nuns?) Directed by Ralph Nelson.

La Dolce Vita—1960. Marcello Mastroianni, Anita Ekberg, Anouk Aimee. Directed by Federico Fellini. The Etiquette Grrls could deal with hanging around in cafes and riding Vespas. Plus, EGL's Mom saw this in Europe in 1960, even though it had been Proclaimed Indecent! EGL's Mom had Moxie!

✓ *Miracle on 34th Street*—1947. Maureen O'Hara, John Payne, Natalie Wood, Edmund Gwenn. If you haven't seen this movie at least twenty-five times by the time *you*, Dear Reader, are twenty-five, there is Something Seriously Wrong with you. Directed by George Seaton.

It's a Wonderful Life—1946. James Stewart, Donna Reed, Lionel Barrymore, Henry Travers. See above. Bert and Ernie from *Sesame Street* got their names from the names of the cop and taxi-driver in this movie. Directed by Frank Capra.

Midnight Cowboy—1969. Jon Voight, Dustin Hoffman. The first movie ever to receive an "X" rating, not to mention the only X-rated picture ever to be nominated for an Academy Award. How indicative of our society and culture in that there is nothing worse in this film than one can find on any current prime-time television show. Note in city crowd scenes that even in 1969, ladies still wore lovely, neat suits and Little White Gloves. Sigh. Directed by John Schlesinger.

✓*The Usual Suspects*—1995. Kevin Spacey, Gabriel Byrne, Stephen Baldwin, Ensemble Cast. A good mystery, and how can anyone not like Kevin Spaccy? Plus, this has a Pretty Damn Good Surprise Ending, too. Directed by Bryan Singer.

The Graduate—1967. Anne Bancroft, Dustin Hoffman, Katharine Ross. We don't care *how* difficult it is to get a ticket to the Broadway Play, the movie is better. Plus, Miss Bancroft manages to be a *WONDERFUL* Mrs. Robinson without Taking It All Off. (And we won't even *SPEAK* to Jason Biggs' and Alicia Silverstone's appearance in the 2002 theatrical production! See our comments on The Theatre below). Fabulous score by Simon & Garfunkel. (We have this on LP, too! We "borrowed" it from the Family Record Collection. Don't tell anyone, Dear Reader!) Directed by Mike Nichols.

Guys and Dolls—1955. Frank Sinatra, Marlon Brando, Jean Simmons, Vivian Blaine. Directed by Joseph L. Mankiewicz. *BRANDO SINGS!!!!!!* ('Nuff said.)

✓*Easy Rider*—1969. Peter Fonda, Dennis Hopper, and a Very Young Jack Nicholson. Directed by Dennis Hopper. Written by Peter Fonda and Dennis Hopper. (Talk about Doing It All Yourself!) A classic, a good soundtrack, and a surprise ending that caught even the Etiquette Grrls by surprise (and we're noted for our skill in seeing a "surprise" ending coming from twenty miles away!). Costumes, amusingly, by Edith Head.

The Music Man—1962. Robert Preston, Shirley Jones, Hermione Gingold, Buddy Hackett, and a Teeny, Tiny Ron Howard. Directed by Morton DaCosta. Musicals like this are What Makes America Great, kats and kittens!

A Room with a View—1986. Helena Bonham Carter, Julian Sands, Daniel Day-Lewis, Rupert Graves. Directed by James Ivory. You can skip all the rest of the Merchant-Ivory films except *The Remains of the Day* (see below) if you watch this one. It will make you need to go to Florence, and it is Funny as All Hell (especially Mr. Day-Lewis as Cecil Le Snip).

✓*Indiana Jones and the Last Crusade*—1989. Harrison Ford, Sean Connery, River Phoenix. Directed by Steven Spielberg. We like all of the Indiana Jones movies, but does it get much better than Indiana Jones going after the Holy Grail? With Sean Connery tagging along for the ride?? No, Dear Reader. It does not.

✓*Monty Python and the Holy Grail*—1975. John Cleese, Eric Idle, Terry Gilliam, etc. Directed by Terry Gilliam and Terry Jones. Well, as shown above, the Etiquette Grrls are Rather Fond of the Holy Grail (and, in our File Cabinets, have the British Literature papers to prove it). But how could anyone not like a film with lines like, "Lobbest thou the Holy Hand Grenade of Antioch toward thy Foe, who, being Naughty in My Sight, shall Snuff It!"

The Remains of the Day—1993. Anthony Hopkins, Emma Thompson, and a very amusing Hugh Grant (before he was Hugh Grant, if you know what we mean). Directed by James Ivory. Based on Kazuo Ishiguro's exquisite novel; will make you want A Full Staff on hand in Your Small Apartment.

Shadowlands—1993. Anthony Hopkins, Debra Winger. Directed by Richard Attenborough. The Etiquette Grrls adore C. S. Lewis. The EGs adore Oxford. The EGs sometimes have a Compelling Urge to watch a film that we *know* will make us Cry Our Eyes Out, and this is pretty darn great for that.

2001: A Space Odyssey—1968. Keir Dullea, Gary Lockwood, William Sylvester. Directed by Stanley Kubrick. Written by Arthur C. Clarke and Kubrick. See this on the Big Screen if at all possible. This film becomes Even More Frightening if you have a troublesome relationship avec Your Computer.

✓*Never Been Kissed*—1999. Drew Barrymore, Michael Vartan, Leelee Sobieski, David Arquette, Molly Shannon. Directed by Raja Gosnell. Yes, it's a bit silly. Yes, it's a Fairy Tale. But if you never fit in with the "cool" kids at school, you must watch this. Plus, that Michael Vartan Fellow is Pretty Darn Cute. None of our English Teachers ever looked like him.

Citizen Kane—1941. Orson Welles. Directed by Orson Welles. Written by Orson Welles. (If you want something done right . . .) Unsurprisingly, loosely based on the life and times of Publishing Behemoth, William Randolph Hearst, who was also keen on the megalomania bit.

Tape—2001. Ethan Hawke, Robert Sean Leonard, Uma Thurman. Sometimes it's really just not A Good Idea to meet up with your old High School pals. It's an even *worse* idea to meet up with them in a seedy motel room in the middle of nowhere. (In fact, it's a good idea to avoid seedy motel rooms in general.) It's a pity that this film was such a limited release, because it's A Damn Good Film. Directed by Richard Linklater.

The Jazz Singer—1927. Al Jolson. Directed by Alan Crosland. The *first* Talking Moving Picture, *ever*. Think about it, Dear Reader. We mean REALLY think about it. How amazing are movies? They're MOVING Pictures that TALK! Isn't that incredible? Think what life would be like without movies . . . isn't that a Horrifying Thought, Dear Reader? (Do *not*, under *any circumstances*, mix this up with the Horrible Neil Diamond Movie of the Same Name [1980].)

Give Our Regards to Broadway

The Etiquette Grrls have been Theatre Buffs for our Entire Lives, and grew up seeing The Best of the Best—Major Stars performing the finest of Drama, Comedy, and Musicals in New York, and London, and Washington, D.C.'s Kennedy Center and Wolf Trap Foundation for the Performing Arts. In fact, if circumstances had been different, the Etiquette Grrls might well have wound up Treading the Boards themselves, but c'est la vie. Here we are at the Etiquette Typewriter, but happy to trot off to the theatre—any theatre—at any and every opportunity! In fact, we love the Dramatic Arts so much, we think it would be far, far easier to tell you What to Avoid when it comes to Theatre than What You Should See, as in our experience, one might see a better high-school production of *Our Town* than a highly touted Broadway Blockbuster.

WHAT TO AVOID

- Anything written after, say, 1965 (there are sometimes exceptions to this rule, but not generally for Musicals).

- Anything by Andrew Lloyd Webber or Stephen Sondheim.

- Anything that pertains to Disney in Any Way Whatsoever.

- Anything with a "score" written by any Pop Star.

- Anything "starring" any former or contemporary Teen Star, unless they are A Real Actor, with Formal Training (e.g., Henry Winkler, despite being best known as *Happy Days'* "The Fonz" is an Enormously Talented, Trained Actor—and a Very Kind, Generous, Polite Man, to boot). Melissa Joan Hart, for example, is *not* An Enormously Talented, Trained Actor. Everyone knows how much the EGs love *90210* (please see page 195 in our first book, *Things You Need to Be Told: A Handbook for Polite Behavior in a Tacky, Rude World!*) but we really, truly *never* want to see any of its stars doing O'Neill. Write to the Etiquette Grrls for Further Details on Real Actors versus Celebrities.

- Anything which advertises on National Television. Like Good Lawyers, Good Plays should not need to Advertise on Television.

- Anything for which Tour Busses arrive by the score, dispelling hordes of poorly dressed tourists. (Who may be spotted by their jeans, sweatshirts, "fanny packs," sensible shoes/sneakers, and their stopping dead in the middle of the sidewalk to take photographs of theatre marquees, Times Square, Macy's, etc., causing People Who Know Where They Are Going to nearly Mow Them Over.)

- Generally speaking, anything that Theatre Critics, especially those from publications like *People* magazine or New York City Tabloid Newspapers, claim to be "SENSATIONAL!"

- With a few exceptions, such as *Show Boat* (from the novel by Edna Ferber), which was blessed with a beautiful score by Jerome Kern (in the 1920s—see the EGs' Theatre Rule Number One), any Serious and/or theretofore Non-Musical Novel/Play/Film that someone has attempted to turn into A Musical. Is *The Poseidon Adventure: The Musical!* a Bad Idea? Yes.

- Likewise, any Major Tragedy that has been turned into a Musical is also In Poor Taste. This includes anything about The Sinking of the *Titanic* or the *Lusitania,* any Famous Earthquake, The Johnstown Flood, The Battle of Gettysburg, or the lives of any Serial Killers.

- Anything which used to be An Opera. A Real Opera, like those which one might see at The Met (or on *Live from Lincoln Center* on television). *La Bohème* (the *real La Bohème,* not Baz Luhrmann's idea of *La Bohème*)=Good. *Rent*=Bad. Yes, some may be un peu dull, but anyone can follow the plotline of any opera

without rock music and/or contemporary dialogue being sub-
stituted for The Real Thing. (Hint: You may find a Plot Sum-
mary in Your Program, plus, these days, there is often a screen
showing subtitles at most classical operas.) The same goes for
Shakespeare. No one should *ever* go see a heavy-metal/valley-
talk version of *Macbeth* set in 1980s' Los Angeles.

- Anything for which the cast must wear/carry Extremely Visible Microphones.

The Etiquette Grrls' Canon of Literature

The Etiquette Grrls are Most Fond of American and British Literature written Between the Wars. (That, Dear Reader, is to say,
between World War I and World War II, lest you thought that we
meant we were Enormous Fans of the literature written between,
say, the Crimean and Boer Wars.) As you know, F. Scott Fitzgerald,
or FSF '17, as we often refer to him, is Our Favorite Writer of All
Time, but this is not to say, Dear Reader, that you should not
familiarize yourself with *all* the Important Authors of *all* genres and
periods. In fact, we'd be simply Thrilled to the Gills if the Editors
of *Norton's Anthology of British* (and/or) *American Literature* were to
ask Our Advice for what should be included in their Next Editions.
However, this is not likely to happen anytime soon, so we ask that
you head to la bibliothèque *RIGHT AWAY* and start reading the
ENTIRE oeuvres of all of the following authors:

- Chaucer—British. Author of *The Canterbury Tales*. If you attend
  one of the EGs' alma mater, you'll have to memorize the
  "Prologue." In Middle English. You may spot any alumna of
  Westover School by the way she pales, and starts quaking in
  her slingbacks anytime she hears the words "Canterbury
  Tales." But, as the Etiquette Grrls' mothers (not to mention
  their English Teachers) say, "What doesn't kill you makes you
  stronger."

- Milton—British. Author of *Paradise Lost*. Another tough one to get through, but you just have to do it, Dear Reader! And any Budding Princeton English Majors had better *like* it!

- William Blake—British. Wrote lots of keen poems, which he gorgeously illustrated himself.

- All of the Romantic Poets (Keats, Shelley, Wordsworth, Byron, etc.)—British. *THE* Poets. They all also led interesting and/or sordid lives, and most died young and tragically . . . it really doesn't get much better than The Romantics, Dear Reader.

✓- William Shakespeare—British. Um . . . He's *Shakespeare!* 'Nuff said.

✓- Ernest Hemingway—American. The Original Mr. Cool Guy. Palled around with the Fitzgeralds, and other ex-pats in France in the 1920s.

✓- F. Scott Fitzgerald—American. FSF. FSF '17. Princeton Alum. Gin-drinker. Icon of The Lost Generation. The EGs' *VERY* Favorite Author of All Time. Author of *The Great Gatsby*. (The EGs' Very Favorite Book of All Time, surprise, surprise.)

- W. Somerset Maugham—British. Author of *Of Human Bondage*. Plus he's got a Cool Name, and he worked as a Secret Agent during WWI!

- Evelyn Waugh—British. Author of *Brideshead Revisited*, which the BBC made into a fabulous mini-series in the early 1980s. The EGs recall watching *Brideshead* on *Masterpiece Theatre* when we were Tiny Tots, and we've been hooked ever since. By the way, in England "Evelyn" is a man's name. We know it's odd. Don't argue, just accept it. Also: pronounced "EVE-lyn," not "EV-eh-lyn." Bit of Trivia: EGL knows firsthand that Mr. Waugh's daughter makes *smashing* Mulled Wine.

✓■ C. S. Lewis—British. Author of *The Chronicles of Narnia*, the first of which is *The Lion, the Witch and the Wardrobe*, and all of which are much, much, *much* better than *any* of those Harry Potter books that the kids are so crazy about these days. Also a very important Catholic Theologian.

■ Nancy Mitford—British. Author of *The Pursuit of Love* and *Love in a Cold Climate*. Loosely based on the life of her family, who were Titled and Pretty Damn Wacky. If the EGs were Young Ladies in 1930s England (which we wish we were), we would be *just* like the characters in these books!

✓■ All of the Brontë Sisters (Charlotte, Anne, and Emily)—British. Authors of *Jane Eyre*, *The Tenant of Wildfell Hall*, and *Wuthering Heights*, respectively. No really decent film has been made of any of these novels, although they are made often. The EGs used to be so obsessed with all things Brontë that we began reading their books in Third Grade. (We were Advanced Readers.)

✓■ Jane Austen—British. Light, fluffy, Comedies of Manners (and Romance), Nineteenth-century Style. We especially like *Sense and Sensibility*, which actually was turned into a decent film version with Emma Thompson (1995). Miss Thompson also wrote the screenplay, which is probably why it's decent—she's such a Clever Lady!

✓■ Beatrix Potter—British. Author and illustrator of *The Tale of Peter Rabbit*, and an entire darling series of wee books about Adorable Animals. If you haven't read these, there is something seriously, seriously wrong with you!

■ Dorothy Parker—American. Author, Poet, Great Wit. Gin-Drinker. Columnist for *Vanity Fair* and *The New Yorker*. Member of the famous Algonquin Round Table. The EGs' Idol and Role Model.

- John-Paul Sartre—French. Existentialist. Author of *No Exit* and that staple of upper-level High School French Classes, *Les Jeux Sont Faits (The Chips Are Down)*. Best read in French. Best re-read sometime *after* you take A.P. French, when you'll be hard-pressed to translate, let alone "get" the Existentialist Angle. Wear all black, listen to jazz, smoke, and drink black coffee while you read.

- Samuel Beckett—Irish (but sometimes wrote in French). Playwright. Proponent of Theatre of the Absurd/Existentialism. Author of *Waiting for Godot,* which is Absolutely Brilliant! (Again, this is something you will want to re-read sometime *after* you are required to read it in High School or College.) EGH was in a production of *Godot* in High School, and still quotes it on a daily basis! In fact, ten years later, she bets she could Run Lines with anyone Right Now! (Brother Joseph, the Director of Theatre at EGH's alma mater, Portsmouth Abbey, always chose *much* more interesting plays for the students than those of the average High School! *And* was enough of a visionary to figure out a way to put a girl into the all-male cast of *Godot*! Wasn't EGH Lucky?)

✓- Carolyn Keene (pseudonym)—American. Author of the Nancy Drew Series. Again, if you haven't read these, you have a Serious, Serious Gap in your childhood, and you *must* read the entire series (except for the new paperback ones, which are rubbish) ASAP! The EGs collect the *Original* Versions (the thick ones with blue-and-orange covers), which were written in the early 1930s. They're about twice the length as newer ones and have beautiful illustrations and Dustjackets (if you're lucky enough to find any with them intact!). The books were rewritten—updated and abridged in the 1940s and '50s (these editions have yellow spines), and both EGs are proud to say that we have a Complete Set of these, handed down from Our Mothers. Nancy is, and always has been a wonderful Role

Model for Girls, and we wholeheartedly reject all of the new feminist "revisionist" readings of the books, which say some very unpleasant things about Nancy and her friends and family. "*BAH!!!!*" we say!!!! Instead, on a Rainy day, when you're suffering from the Mean Reds, curl up with a Nancy Mystery, some Hot Chocolate, and some Cookies, and you'll feel much, much better—we promise you!

- Franklin W. Dixon (pseudonym)—American. Author of the Hardy Boys Series. See above, only this series was meant for Boys. But the EGs read them, too—how could we resist books about well-mannered, handsome, clever boys who dash about Solving Mysteries! We're also the Proud Owners of the rare *Hardy Boys Detective Handbook,* from which we learned How to Lift Fingerprints, and other Sleuthing Techniques. This, Dear Reader, is just *one* reason why the Etiquette Grrls are not to be trifled with.

- Eugene O'Neill—American. Playwright. And not just *any* playwright, but the EGs' Very Favorite Playwright! Plus, both EGH and EGL were once in a production of *Ah, Wilderness!,* one of O'Neill's Lighter Works.

- Kay Thompson—American. Actress. Chanteuse. Author of *Eloise*. Need we say more?

✓ - Agatha Christie—British. Greatest mystery novelist of All Time.

- Christopher Buckley—American. Portsmouth Abbey Alumnus. Son of William F. Buckley (he of the Enviable Vocabulary). Humorist. Essayist. Novelist. Frequent contributor to *The New Yorker* magazine, to which you should subscribe.

- Dominick Dunne—American. Novelist. Crusader for Justice. Contributor to *Vanity Fair* (another magazine you should be reading). Start with *A Season in Purgatory*, the EGs' Very Favorite of Mr. Dunne's novels!

- P. J. O'Rourke—American. Humorist. Essayist. Has a marvelous way of making Politics très amusant, regardless of Your Affiliation. Plus, Mr. O'Rourke is the author of an uproariously funny satiric etiquette book, *Modern Manners*, which was a Great Influence on the EGs.

- Patricia Highsmith—American. Author of the Ripley novels and many short stories. See above for the EGs' take on the film version of *The Talented Mr. Ripley*.

- J. D. Salinger—American. Known for Being Reclusive, and, oh yeah, also for writing *The Catcher in the Rye*, one of the EGs' Favorite Books of All Time.

- Kurt Vonnegut—American. Author of *Cat's Cradle, Slaughterhouse-Five*, and much more.

- Douglas Adams—British. Author of *The Hitchhiker's Guide to the Galaxy*, wherein you will learn The Answer to Life, the Universe, and Everything. (Can you expect anything more, Dear Reader?)

- Charles Dickens—British. Dear Reader, if you manage to get out of High School without having the introduction to *A Tale of Two Cities* branded into your memory forever, you're quite the Anomaly.

- L. M. Montgomery—Canadian. Best known as author of the Anne of Green Gables series, but also wrote many other wonderful Children's Books. EGH and EGL look like Anne and Diana, and we're un peu Peevish, Still, that the middle-school production didn't Cast Us In These Roles. Hmmpf.

✓▪ Beverly Cleary—American. Author of the Ramona books, the mention of which can still send the EGs into Fits of Giggles. "Jesus, Beezus!"

✓▪ Ayn Rand—American. *The Fountainhead* is undoubtedly her Best Work. Don't get too caught up with the Ideas of Objectivism, though, or you'll resemble an over-zealous High School Senior whose idol, until discovering Ayn Rand, was Trent Reznor.

▪ Jack Kerouac—American. If you're planning on taking a Road Trip anytime in your life, *On the Road* is Required Reading.

▪ James Joyce—Irish. Even though EGL got a little tired of being asked to give the "Irish Catholic Perspective" on every single plot element in *A Portrait of the Artist as a Young Man* in her high-school English class, both of us still love Joyce.

▪ Henry James—American. Author of lovely, lovely novels that one must read Quite Slowly, so as to savor every turn of phrase.

▪ D. H. Lawrence—British. Best known for Novels that were considered Racy, Back in the Day. You should read Lawrence's short stories, too—they're Often Overlooked.

✓ Louisa May Alcott—Prolific Concord, Massachusetts–based author of *Little Women, Little Men, Jo's Boys,* etc. We dare you not to get choked up when Beth dies.

✓▪ Edgar Allan Poe—American. He was Goth, Dear Reader, before Goth Was Cool.

▪ Henry David Thoreau—Another famous resident of Concord, Massachusetts. If you go to Walden Pond, you can see a replica of his Wee Cabin, which is about the size of a Decent Walk-In Closet, these days.

- William Faulkner—American. Let it not be said that the EGs do not like Southern Writers!

- Tennessee Williams—American. Oh, Dear Reader, you must read *The Glass Menagerie*. Then you must seek out a Good Stage Production of it, *STAT!*

✓ Dr. Seuss—American. Pseudonym of one Theodor Geisel. Every child should have every last one of his books!

- Flannery O'Connor—American. *A Good Man Is Hard to Find* is smashing, and, well, we couldn't Agree More avec the Title.

- G. K. Chesterton—British. Author of the Father Brown mysteries. Theologian, too.

- Raymond Chandler—American, raised in Britain. Creator of Philip Marlowe; author of really, really keen mysteries, including *The Big Sleep*. You haven't read a Real Mystery unless you've read one of Chandler's, or one by . . .

✓ Dashiell Hammett—American. Creator of Sam Spade; author of brilliant mysteries, including *The Thin Man* and *The Maltese Falcon*.

- Nathaniel Hawthorne—American. You won't get through a Pre–Civil War American Lit class without becoming extremely familiar avec Mr. Hawthorne. Tip: Hester Prynne makes a Top-Drawer Halloween Costume!

- Alfred, Lord Tennyson—British. If you read nothing else of his, read "Ulysses."

✓ Mary Shelley—British. Author of *Frankenstein*, a novel that really deserves to be read, especially if you think you Already Understand the whole idea of the Monster.

✓ Bram Stoker—Irish. As with *Frankenstein*, Stoker's novel *Dracula* has, sadly, been Largely Forgotten as the main character became a pop culture fixture. Trust the EGs: Unless you've got a Couple of Hours on your hands, you do *not* want to get EGL into a conversation about how this novel gives an excellent perspective on Fin de Siècle British Societal Fears.

- Thornton Wilder—American. *Our Town* is The Bee's Knees, but *Theophilus North* is our favorite.

- The Rossettis (D. G. and Christina), and all other Pre-Raphaelites—British. If you want a good perspective on Pre-Raphaelite Art, you must read these writers' works.

- Oscar Wilde—British. *The Importance of Being Earnest* is, simply, one of the Funniest Plays to have ever been written.

- Vladimir Nabokov—Russian; later lived in Europe and the U.S. Yes, *Lolita* is Un Peu Creepy, but it's crafted so perfectly.

- Walt Whitman—American. Although, if we hear one more poet called "Whitman-esque" just because he uses long lines of Free Verse, we're going to scream!

- Anton Chekhov—Russian. The EGs think someone should put together a really good production of *The Cherry Orchard* right now, because it's been a while since we've seen it. In a pinch, though, reading it will do.

- ✓ Mark Twain—American. While we're sure you encountered Mr. Twain in A.P. English, you should give him another chance.

- Edith Wharton—American. You should read all of her fiction as well as her writing on Interior Design. Come to think of it, most people who Fancy Themselves Interior Designers these days should be forced to Copy Out, in their Best Penmanship, every single word Dear Edith ever wrote on the subject.

- Lisa Birnbach—American. C'mon, you've heard of *The Official Preppy Handbook*!

✓ Ludwig Bemelmans—Austrian. Remember Madeline?

✓ E. B. White—American. Have questions about the EGs' Random Capitalization? Mr. White is one of the Forbears of this Great Tradition.

- T. S. Eliot—American who tried to Become British. One must always be able to drop the appropriate line from "The Love Song of J. Alfred Prufrock" into Conversation, so one must, ergo, read Eliot.

- Julia Child—American. Okay, so she wrote Cookbooks, but you should read them anyway.

- Anthony Burgess—British. *A Clockwork Orange* will give you a Whole New Patois!

- David Sedaris—American. Funny as All Hell.

Oh, hell, Dear Reader—we can't list Everybody. (Sigh.) Just go to The Library and Read Everything. Well, perhaps not *everything* . . . feel free to Pass By *The Rules*, etc.

"With a Song in My Heart": The Composers, Songwriters, Lyricists, Bands, and Singers You Should Know

THE CLASSICAL COMPOSERS

- Bach, Beethoven, Brahms, and all the other Classical Guys. (You can skip all twentieth-century ones, though, like Whatshisname and his "Tonal Poetry," which strikes us as actually being Pretty Darn Atonal, and, thus, Pretty Darn Excruciating to listen to.)

THE TWENTIETH-CENTURY SONGWRITERS

- Les Frères Gershwin (George wrote the music, Ira wrote the lyrics)

- Irving Berlin

- Rodgers and Hart (Rodgers—composer, Hart—lyricist)

- Rodgers and Hammerstein (same Rodgers; Hart Bought the Farm at an Early Age, sadly; Hammerstein—lyricist)

- Jerome Kern

- Harold Arlen

- Johnny Mercer

THE DANCE BANDS

- Glenn Miller (lead trombone)

- Benny Goodman (lead clarinet)

- Artie Shaw (lead clarinet)

- Gene Krupa (lead drums)

- Bix Beiderbecke (lead cornet)

- Bunny Berigan (lead trumpet, a favorite of EGH's Mom)

- Tommy and Jimmy Dorsey (trombone, sax, clarinet; they each had their own bands)

- Lionel Hampton (lead vibraphone)

- Billy May (also arranger of many Sinatra and Darin albums)

- Bob Crosby (der Bingle's Brother—see below)

- Louis Prima (composer, lyricist, singer; not to be confused with Mr. Jordan)

- Louis Jordan (composer, lyricist, singer; not to be confused with Mr. Prima)

- Lester Lanin. One simply can*not* make One's Debut, or have any sort of Society dance without him!

- Paul Whiteman. Ditto.

THE GREAT SINGERS

✔- Frank Sinatra (Chairman of the Board)

- Dean Martin

- Ella Fitzgerald

- Billie Holiday

- Count Basie

- Peggy Lee

- Rosemary Clooney (George's aunt)

- Bing Crosby

✔ - Louis Armstrong (Terrific Trumpet Player, too!)

- Etta James

- Al Jolson (appeared in first "talking picture," i.e., movie; see page 95)

- Edith Piaf

- Chet Baker (also trumpet player)

- Harry Connick, Jr. (also composer, lyricist, pianist, former Child Prodigy, occasional actor, to whom the EGs were listening in Ninth Grade, when Everyone Else was obsessed with New Kids on the Block. And EGH met Harry Senior, the then–District Attorney of New Orleans after a concert at Albert Hall in London. He was Über-keen!!!)

- Nat King Cole

- Michael Feinstein (also pianist)

- John Pizzarelli (also guitarist)

ROCK AROUND THE CLOCK

✓ ▪ Elvis Presley (The King)

- Ricky Nelson (son of Ozzie and Harriet)

- Buddy Holly

✓ The Beatles

✓ The Beach Boys

✓ Patsy Cline

- U2

✓ Radiohead

- Cake (the Etiquette Grrls' Favorite Contemporary Band)

- Simon and Garfunkel

- Big Bad Voodoo Daddy (well, not Rock exactly, but Swing Revivalists; please note that the band's name is *singular*)

- Bobby Darin (was married to Sandra Dee)

- Violent Femmes

- Herb Alpert and the Tijuana Brass

- The Clash

- The Cure

✓ Red Hot Chili Peppers

- Garbage

- Beck

✓ Bob Dylan

- Bill Haley and the Comets

- Lesley Gore (to whom we raise a glass simply because she must have endured the same Constant Misspellings of Her First Name that ECL does)

✓ Coldplay

- The Pogues

✓ The Wallflowers

- Smash Mouth

✓ Wilco

✓ The Sex Pistols

✓ The Rolling Stones

- Marianne Faithfull

- Dusty Springfield

- Dick Dale and the Del-Tones

- Dion (with and without the Belmonts)—named after Belmont Avenue in the Bronx, which runs along the boundary of Fordham University, where EGH went to school her Freshman Year, *not* Belmont, Massachusetts, where EGL lived for a couple of years

- The Crew Cuts (clean-cut Doo-Wop group of the '50s; sang EGH's Mom's favorite Rock and Roll–era song, "Sh-boom." Pretty Damn Catchy!)

✓ - Barenaked Ladies

✓ - The Pixies

- The Kingston Trio

- Don McLean

- Roger Miller

✓ Johnny Cash (well, technically, he's Country, but he's *Old* Country, and that's okay)

- Glen Campbell (another decent Old Country/Rock sort)

- Fats Domino

- The Mama & the Papas

- The Monkees

✓ - Van Morrison

✓ - R.E.M.

- Neil Sedaka

- Connie Francis

✓ - The Supremes

- Petula Clark

- Sergio Mendez and Brasil 66

- The Lovin' Spoonful

- The Everly Brothers

- Sam Cooke

- Brian Setzer and His Orchestra/The Stray Cats

✓ ▪ Eve6

- Kittyhawk

- The Buggles (because their video for "Video Killed the Radio Star" was the First Video Shown on MTV, and you will need to know their name at Some Cocktail Party, Somewhere, when someone mentions this)

- Aimee Mann

- Rufus Wainwright

- Paul Williams (responsible for the soundtrack of *The Muppet Movie*, including "The Rainbow Connection," which is one of the EGs' Favorite Songs *ever*)

- They Might Be Giants

- Smashing Pumpkins

✓ ▪ Nirvana (you don't have to like them, or their Flannel Shirts, but you must Know Who They Are)

Art for Art's Sake: Art History 101

Well, Dear Reader, the Etiquette Grrls could teach an Introductory Course in the History of Art, but as you know, we're Un Peu Verbose, and think we'd have some problems condensing All the Important Material into one or two Pithy Paragraphs. Thus, we will leave you with some Simple Advice:

1. Go to the Metropolitan Museum of Art in New York City.

2. Look at Everything.

3. Be sure to read the labels (blurbs) on the wall next to each object.

Be forewarned that this may take days, weeks, or even an Entire Lifetime.

Going Dancing

The Etiquette Grrls aren't at all wild about the Club Scene, if truth be told. We don't see the sense in standing in line for ages and paying Outrageous Cover Fees only to acquire Pounding Headaches from techno music or get trampled to death in a Mosh Pit. However, we enjoy good music, and like wearing pretty clothes—thus, for us, swing's the thing.

IT DON'T MEAN A THING IF IT AIN'T GOT THAT SWING

The Etiquette Grrls are simply Thrilled To The Gills that there's been such a tremendous resurgence in swing music and dancing! When we were Tiny Tots and most of our peers were busy doing the Hokey-Pokey and the Bunny Hop, we would roll back the oriental rugs in our parents' living rooms and practice the Lindy to the strains of Benny Goodman and Glenn Miller until we dropped from Exhaustion. However, while we think it's grand that so many young people are content to jitterbug the night away in lieu of ungracefully thrashing around to techno music at raves, we have discovered that even the most uncoordinated people seem to be under the impression that they are splendid swing dancers and should attempt highly acrobatic dance moves, such as those in the famous ad for khakis from a Well-Known Clothing Store. The Etiquette Grrls sincerely doubt that you are The Lord of The Swing, and, thusly, you should not, most especially on a crowded dance floor, attempt to toss your dance partner over your head and consequently into a wall, as this may well result in a broken arm and numerous other injuries. We remind you that you should not interpret the "wail" of "Jump, Jive, and Wail" as license to cause bodily harm to others. Should you wish to be beaten, or to beat others to a Bloody Pulp during your evenings out on the town, Dear Reader, we suggest that you go find a lovely Wee Mosh Pit.

"SAVE ME THE WALTZ": OTHER THOUGHTS ON DANCING

How it grieves the Etiquette Grrls that no one seems to know how to dance properly these days! Everyone, but *everyone,* should familiarize themselves with the basics of traditional dances such as the waltz, two-step, and fox-trot. Now, we're not suggesting that you must dash out to Arthur Murray and style yourself as the next Fred Astaire or Ginger Rogers (who, it has been famously noted, had to do everything Fred did, only backward and in high heels— quite a feat, and not Just Another Rhumba, indeed!), but you should familiarize yourself with all the basic dances, such as the fox-trot and waltz, which will, at the very least, come in handy at Your Cotillion Ball and Wedding Reception. There truly is Nothing Worse than seeing a bride getting impossibly tangled in her dress as her father/husband/whoever attempts to drag her around the dance floor because she doesn't know how to fox-trot with a reasonable degree of Grace and Style. Which brings us to another point. The *only* appropriate music for receptions and cotillions is that of the Traditional Variety—that is to say, classic songs from the 1930s and '40s. (If you want to be *truly* old-school, you must hire Lester Lanin's band, which has played at every debutante ball and wedding reception worth attending since The Dawn Of Time. And as a bonus, you'll get Darling Little Beanies as party favors.) Under no circumstances may you have any disco, country, heavy metal, "Top 40" (especially *anything* by Celine Dion or Whitney Houston), or alternative rock. (Although the Etiquette Grrls do *love* alternative rock in its place, there's nothing worse than an "easy listening" cover version of a Garbage song.) Nor may you play any song that will encourage anyone to do the Electric Slide, the Macarena, or any variety of so-called "Line Dancing." In moments of informality, the Etiquette Grrls will allow you to do The Twist (which became dignified and ceased to be a mere teenage fad when First Lady Betty Ford twisted the night away to "Bad, Bad Leroy Brown" at the 1976 Republican National Convention), which is easy, fun, has been around long enough to be considered traditional, and is danced to catchy early '60s tunes, such as those sung by the very hip swinger Bobby Darin. In fact, Dear Reader, peruse the racks of your local used record store, and you'll find that everybody, but *everybody*, from Lester Lanin to Mae West made a Twist Album in the early 1960s. Collect them all, and Twist the Night Away!

Television

The Etiquette Grrls are usually so busy gadding about town that we don't often watch much television. Which isn't necessarily a Bad Thing, as there isn't much worthwhile on these days anyway. Of all the shows currently on Network Television, we really only care for *The West Wing* and *Law & Order*. Naturally, you should also watch the national, world, and local news nightly in order to keep abreast of Current Events, both on the Large (e.g., Impending War) and Small (e.g., A Serial Killer on the loose in Your Neighborhood) Scale. Believe us, Dear Reader, you will be able to Survive Life if you don't watch *Friends*. However, you *should* have a vague inkling of at least the premise and the stars of Classic Television Shows, like *M*A*S*H*, and *The Brady Bunch*, and *Perry Mason*. Make Nick at Nite and TV Land Your Friends. For, Dear Reader, if you are making Small Talk at a cocktail party, and talk turns to, say, James Garner in *The Rockford Files* versus James Garner in *Maverick*, you will sound and look like a new arrival from Outer Space if you've never heard of these shows, and *especially* if you haven't the slightest idea who Mr. Garner is! Also, Classic TV is the root of many Famous Catchphrases, which you probably use All the Time, such as "Sorry about that, Chief," "And . . . *loving* it!" and "Missed it by *that* much!" (*Get Smart*), "Verrrrrrrry In-ter-es-ting . . ." and "Here come da judge!" and "You bet your bippy!" (*Rowan and Martin's Laugh-In*), "Just the facts, ma'am" (*Dragnet*), "SCHNELL!" (*Hogan's Heroes*), "Submitted for your approval . . ." (*The Twilight Zone*), "Book 'em, Dano!" (*Hawaii Five-O*), and "Your Mission, should you choose to accept it . . ." (*Mission: Impossible*). Of course,

Dear Reader, we're not saying that TV Land is the *OED*, but, really, one ought to have a vague idea of the etymology of one's favorite words and phrases!

As bad as most television shows are, we've noticed that Daytime Television is Particularly Loathsome. Intelligent, well-bred people do not watch Soap Operas or Trashy "Talk" Shows where the guests, or worse, The Host, are likely to engage in A Brawl of Any Sort. Fortunately, as the Etiquette Grrls are Frail Creatures, and are quite often At Home During the Day, we've noticed that if one is clever, one may watch *Law & Order* nearly continuously throughout the day and night, which is acceptable. We don't know why someone doesn't just start a *Law & Order* Channel (LOC) in order to save us all from all that channel-flipping!

As with Network Television, the Vast Majority of Cable Television is Rather Loathsome—we wish that when signing up for Cable (as one must in many, many locations merely to receive good reception of network television), one could simply choose the channels one wanted, and do away with the Home Shopping Network and so forth. EG-approved Cable Channels include: Nick at Nite and TV Land (as mentioned above), AMC (American Movie Classics), TMC (Turner Movie Classics), TNT (only for movies, *The X-Files*, and *Law & Order*), A&E, Sci-Fi (for old *Twilight Zone* and *Outer Limits* episodes, and the occasional Good Movie, like *Gattaca*), FX (for reruns of *90210*, *M*A*S*H*, etc.), Bravo (we love *Inside the Actors' Studio*), VH1 (for *Behind the Music*—very good viewing when one is Un Peu Hungover), CNN, and Headline News. PBS should, of course, be A Staple of your Television-Watching Diet. How could anyone survive without *Antiques Roadshow*, *Mystery!*, *Masterpiece Theatre*, and *This Old House*?!

Sporting Events

The Etiquette Grrls, if truth be told, are not très sportives. The only forms of sporting activity in which we actively participate are rather mild, easily understood, and not terribly likely to dirty our clothes, such as croquet, golf, and badminton. The Etiquette Grrls play a Rather Vicious Game of Badminton, as a matter of fact, and will readily crush most of our opponents. However, we are Polite Victors and always shake hands with and buy a round of drinks for our Vanquished Foes, and we recommend that you follow this example, whatever your sport of choice may be.

It is very rude to attempt to force a nonathletic type to play a sport, especially in public. If your friend demurs when you invite her to join your traditional family game of touch football, do not press her. She may not understand the rules, and does not want to embarrass herself; she may have an Injury; she may have just had her nails manicured and does not want to chip them. She may even have refused because she is Terribly Good at the sport, and would surpass your own skills. For example, while the Etiquette Grrls loathe volleyball, one of them happens, by mere chance, to possess an extremely fast, accurate, deadly overhead serve. Forcing this Etiquette Grrl to join a game, and snickering while she is preparing to serve, will most likely result in your Getting the Wind Knocked Out of You due to the impact of a Volleyball avec Your Torso. So beware, buster! Some Truly Polite People demur for fear of embarrassing *you,* and you can never tell this by just looking at them, so you should always let them sit out the game if they wish.

If your guests do join you, you should not forget to fill them in on any odd House Rules you have for the sport. Your guests do not know, and it is rude to deceive them. And remember that some sports are never, *ever* fun for anyone, and if you invite others to join you in pursuing them, they will most likely shun your company in the future. We've listed common perceptions of several "popular" sports below; you may want to reconsider your own participation in them:

Hunting: Involves firearms, which, like the Etiquette Grrls, are Not to Be Trifled With. Furthermore, Small and Furry Animals often are killed by hunters, and killing Small and Furry Animals is Rude.

If you are hell-bent on killing something smaller than you, we suggest you stick to Vile Creatures like spiders or creepy-crawly things you find in the sink in the summertime. Fox should never, ever, ever be hunted, because they are Extremely Cute. Fox-hunting apparel is the only real reason to go hunting, and if you really want to wear this stuff, dress as a hunter for Halloween. Besides, surely you are not Quite So Destitute or so Far from Civilization that you must kill your own food, right? If this is true, Dear Reader, you should either get a better job or move.

Wrestling: Oh, please. We won't even go into the "professional" aspect of this, as it's Beneath Us. But even high-school wrestling is To Be Avoided. The uniforms flatter no one, and the Etiquette Grrls think that boys "trying to make weight" is really rather silly. Why would anyone want to partake in any sort of activity that requires one to drastically alter one's Normal Eating Patterns?

Fishing: If the Etiquette Grrls wanted to get up at an ungodly hour and sit in a boat, they would obviously Row. We don't even want to do that, really, but crew at least is Preppy, and does not involve such horrors as Live, Angry Fish. Also see our last statement on hunting, above. But at least fishing, the Etiquette Grrls understand, is a quiet, non-sweaty sort of sport, and that's one tiny little thing in its favor.

Running/jogging/track: Surely you, like the Etiquette Grrls, can get enough exercise while you are shopping? Dear Reader, if you must run in public, do not *ever* wear a vile sweatsuit (and all sweatsuits are by nature vile), and don't get in the way of our Volvo. If you run at night or in foul weather or if we can pass you while we're walking, you should know you Will Be Laughed At, and deservedly so. Perhaps most importantly, if you *do* go out for a run, you should take Great Pains not to Mow Down any pedestrians sauntering along at a more leisurely pace. Also, you should not make the sidewalk of The Main Thoroughfare of Your City or Town part of Your Route!

Basketball: Even though, like the Etiquette Grrls, it is From New England, it is boring and often THOR (unlike the Etiquette Grrls). Unless it's Princeton, in which case, you may watch.

Auto or motorcycle racing: Boring and pointless. Exactly what is sporting about driving in a circle? Nevertheless, the Etiquette Grrls have One Good Thing to say about racing: We understand that Paul Newman, the Famous Actor, is a Rather Good Race Car Driver, and we think that Mr. Newman is Grand. Also, if one *must* follow Auto Racing, Formula One is far preferable to NASCAR, as Formula One Races have been held ever since there were, like, automobiles (as we recall, Chitty Chitty Bang Bang was a Retired Formula One Race Car), and the races are held in Keen Places like the Actual Streets of Monte Carlo.

Bowling: Should never, ever be taken seriously. You do not go to a bowling alley more than once per year, and you should only go in the company of a group of people who are, like you, just interested in slumming for an evening. You should drink a lot of cheap beer, about which you should complain, you should not know how to work the score projector (because to know would indicate you've been bowling before), and you should make jokes about the Serious Bowlers in the other lanes (but not loud enough that they'll slash the tires on your wee Mercedes). Under no circumstances should you own your own bowling ball!!! Only people who would obviously never be caught dead in a bowling alley should go to one—poets make particularly excellent companions. Furthermore, as it's From New England, Candlepin Bowling is infinitely cooler than the kind with the big ball.

Any Sport That Bills Itself As "Extreme": Steer clear, and let Natural Selection do its important work.

Although the Etiquette Grrls are not keen on Professional Sports, even we admit that once in a while attending a game might be sort of enjoyable, especially if you live in a city that is Particularly Fond of their team (as in the way that Bostonians feel about the Red Sox). And there is, we admit, something soothingly All-American about a good, old-fashioned baseball game on a lazy summer afternoon, and exciting about the fast-paced nature of a hockey match. (Incidentally, the Etiquette Grrls, who can't even *stand up* on skates, are rather astonished that anybody could play a game that requires such Quick Reflexes on them!) What we most object to is not the game itself, but rather, the all-too-common rudeness among the fans. This, fortunately, is something that we feel can be easily remedied. People frequently look and act like the idiots they are, and this is sad, a symptom of the Decline of Society. However, Dear Reader, you do not have to sink to this level. Remember, you can always cheer your favorite team on to victory *without* being rude or looking foolish. Never, ever:

- Paint, draw, stencil, or tattoo a team logo, name, mascot, etc., on any part of your body, particularly a part of your body that should obviously not be exposed in public.

- Purchase an "official game jersey" bearing the name and number of your favorite player, and wear it in public before, during, and after the game. Are you *really* Ray Bourque? The Etiquette Grrls think not.

- Bring props—a big foam #1 finger, cheese hat, pom-poms, cowbell, etc.

- Make a sign. Well-bred people do not really want to see their faces projected on a stadium scoreboard. Signs with misspellings and Grammar Mistakes are Particularly Annoying.

- Throw anything at the players, referees, or at other fans, unless it's a Frighteningly Clever Thing that will not hurt anybody it should hit. Octopi, fish, oranges, tomatoes, hats, paper airplanes, etc., have all been done. In fact, it is *generally* unkind to throw things at people, no matter where you are.

- Act as if the team you favor chose to play poorly simply as an affront to you and you alone, and sulk for days.

- Spill your beer. Sporting Events are so annoying, Dear Reader, that you should be sucking down that beer in an effort to mentally escape having to watch the game, or more likely, mentally escape the fans who are not as polite as you are, Dear Reader, and who are Driving You To Distraction. In any case, your beer should not be sitting around long enough for you to spill it.

- Jump up and down in place if you're seated on bleachers. If enough people follow you, you may all die in A Horrible Bleacher Collapse, but that's what you get for being a lemming, and don't say we didn't warn you.

We should say that in the spectrum of Sporting Events, college sports are always more entertaining than Professional Sports. Of course, everyone adores cheering on their Alma Mater, and if your school is not quite a Sports Powerhouse, well, maybe it just makes them all the more endearing. Also, the Etiquette Grrls have a certain degree of, dare we say, fondness, for college sports, because it makes us think of the Good Old Days, when all the girls from the Seven Sisters, and perhaps also from Miss Porter's and Westover, in their nice little tweed suits and furs, went down by train to New Haven for the big Harvard-Yale game, and there was a Formal, and a whole *round* of elegant parties, and a Smashing Time was had by all. Oh, how we wish things were still like the Glory Days,

Dear Reader! If this were so, the Etiquette Grrls might even be enticed to attend college football games regularly!

SPORTS THAT THE ETIQUETTE GRRLS RATHER LIKE (AND ACTUALLY PLAY THEMSELVES)

- **Badminton**—Only played in the Backyard, preferably avec Wooden Racquets and the old-fashioned Birdies.

- **Riding**—English saddle only. And preferably dans England itself, for that matter. Riding in The English Countryside is Utterly Smashing; riding around a hot and dusty indoor rink in Vermont is Not So Smashing. And while Riding itself is a lovely skill to possess, the EGs have never understood Some People's Obsession avec Horses. If you're over twelve and *Black Beauty* is still your very favorite book, you should take up some Other Hobbies.

- **Sailing**—The Etiquette Grrls mean Actual Sailing, not Zipping About in Motorboats. And sailing dans The Ocean, not Some Pond somewhere.

- **Tennis**—Only if you can be A Lady or Gentleman about it. As the British Tennis Coach at one Etiquette Grrl's Prep School wrote of that Etiquette Grrl, "Etiquette Grrl was a pleasure to be around, chatty and cheerful in every class, and was an example to everyone of how to behave on a tennis court. It is a shame that more of the 'tennis brats' do not follow her example." Also, remember, Dear Reader, Tennis Whites are Just That—no Other Colors, *ever*! Also, Your Tennis Outfits should not be So Skimpy that they could be mistaken for A Bathing Suit, particularly when playing at, say Wimbledon, or The Casino in Newport. When Hitting The Ball Around, the Etiquette Grrls always wear Modest White Piqué Dresses. Vintage Tennis Dresses are Keen! We also carry

Wooden Racquets. Do we need oversized, über-lightweight titanium racquets to Hit the Ball? No, we do not, thank you very much.

- **Hockey, Ice**—Well, of course, the Etiquette Grrls don't actually *play* Hockey—that would be Very Unladylike. But it is sort of Exciting to Watch, we must admit.

- **Hockey, Field**—Naturally, the Etiquette Grrls haven't been on a Playing Field since they Left School, and perhaps it's a bit of an Overstatement to say that the Etiquette Grrls *like* Field Hockey, but it does make us un peu nostalgic for the Halcyon Days of Girls' School. Plus, any sport which requires you to wear cute little kilts can't be all bad.

- **Skeet Shooting**—One of the few times when Firearms are Posh.

- **Golf**—If you belong to the Über-Swanky Carnegie Club, you can go and stay at Skibo, Andrew Carnegie's Castle in Scotland. The EGs would like to remind you, however, that you are not Tiger Woods, and there is no need to purchase Giant, Terribly Expensive, Super-Powerful Metal "Woods" or Irons that feature better technology than the Stealth Bomber. Your mother's or father's old set of Clubs, preferably in their old Golf Bag, will do Just Fine.

- **Croquet**—Avail yourself of a Really Good Set (not one of those Cutesy-Pie kiddie ones), and drink Pink Lemonade.

- **Lounging on the Lanai by The Pool**—The Etiquette Grrls will have another Mai Tai, please!

It should be noted that unless you are a Professional Athlete (e.g., Your Main Source of Income is from your Athletic Endeavors), it is Positively THOR to play *any* sport for any reason other than for pure pleasure. Adults do not play Competitive

Sports, nor do they play for "keeps." Ladies and Gentlemen may certainly play a round of tennis, but it doesn't matter who wins, because you'll all sit around and have a big pitcher of Pimm's afterward without any Nasty Grudges.

Questions and Answers on Various and Sundry

Dear Etiquette Grrls,

Promptly on Labor Day, I put away my white shoes and my straw hats and handbags, just as I knew you'd like me to. But what about open-toed shoes and sleeveless clothes? What about linen? My Dear Mother raised me never to wear any of these things after Labor Day, and I simply can't bring myself to do otherwise! But the thing is, Dear Etiquette Grrls, I live in the Deep South, and it's 97 degrees today (as it is wont to be for the entire Autumn)! Am I being Stodgy? What say you, dear Etiquette Grrls?

Sincerely,
Scorching in the South

Dear Scorching,

The Etiquette Grrls know all too well that it stays Pretty Toasty down South well into, say, February. Obviously, we expect our Dear Readers to exercise a wee bit of common sense when it comes to Their Autumn Wardrobe—what's appropriate garb for Northern Climes in the early Autumn is simply Not Feasible for someone living in The Deep South. Of course, Dear Reader, if you live Deep in the Heart of Texas, you shouldn't prance about in Harris Tweed and Shetland Sweaters come September! Heavens, we wouldn't want all our Dear Southern Readers to collectively Die of Heatstroke!!

The Etiquette Grrls don't see why their Dear Southern Readers should be Overly Hasty when packing away the sleeveless dresses

and sandals. We would, however, put away our Straw Hats and
Handbags and any White Shoes (not that the Etiquette Grrls ac-
tually own any White Shoes!), as you have already done, Dear
Reader. We'd also put our White Piqué Dresses, as well as anything
else that Positively Screams Summer that might be floating around
in the Far Reaches of the closet. (And we encourage all of our Dear
Old-Fashioned Southern Boy Readers to put away their adorable
Seersucker Suits and Straw Boaters!)

Instead of Overtly Summery Clothes or Heavy Woolens, the
Etiquette Grrls recommend that you, Dear Southern Reader, wear
things that are lightweight (even Linen is okay, if it's Very Warm),
but in Autumnal Colors. For example, you could wear a pumpkin-
colored linen, cotton, or silk shift dress, with brown shoes—slides
or sandals would be all right for informal day wear—and a Brown
Leather Handbag. You'll still be able to stay cool, but not look Out
of Season!

Warm regards,
The Etiquette Grrls

Dear Etiquette Grrls,

*How should a lady style her hair? Is it simply a matter of being tasteful
and convenient? I have very long hair, you see, and am concerned that I
may not be making a Proper Impression by leaving it to hang down my
back.*

Rapunzel

Dear Rapunzel,

Well, to an extent, it's more a matter of How You Act With
Your Hair than How Long It Is. Everyone needs to stop playing
with their hair right now! Everyone! Especially if you are anywhere
near Food or if you are in any sort of Remotely Formal Setting!
(There is almost nothing worse than someone who undergoes a

Job Interview whilst flipping a lock of hair around in her hand!) Also, try to avoid having your hair invade Other People's Personal Space. If you frequently need to lean over someone's computer screen at work, for example, and your hair falls onto that person's face, you should consider keeping your hair pulled up or back during the workday. Moreover, once one is Not A Schoolgirl, it seems Less Than Sophisticated to have Long, Golden Locks hanging down your back. It's just Not Polished, and particularly in an Office Setting, you may find that people do not Take You Seriously. There are many simple and attractive ways to wear your hair up, Dear Reader, and the Etiquette Grrls really think you'd be better off doing so at the office.

Sincerely yours,
The Etiquette Grrls

Dear Etiquette Grrls,

I am hoping that perhaps such cultured and stylish Ladies as yourselves could help solve a Fashion Dilemma that I'm having. What does one wear to an absolutely Thrilling Evening avec one's husband to sit through countless hours of Wagnerian opera at the Met?

Warmest regards,
Die Walküre

Dear Die Walküre,

The Etiquette Grrls believe you may be our first Correspondent avec an Umlaut in her Pen Name! The Etiquette Grrls simply adore Umlauts! (Indeed, doesn't everyone?) But we digress. We don't think you could go wrong treating the Opera as a Formal Occasion . . . you could really Pull Out All the Stops. Or, of course, this would be a Perfect Opportunity for your Little Black Dress and Your Pearls.

We don't think that Wagnerian Opera really requires any different sort of Dress Code than Opera In General, despite the fact that Wagnerian Opera generally goes on for Days, it seems. However, the Etiquette Grrls have, indeed, gotten Rather Silly thinking of Accessories One Might Bring to a Wagnerian Opera, if Wagnerian Opera followed the same sort of rules as, say, the Rocky Horror Picture Show. Perhaps a Cunningly Decorated Beer Stein might be In Order! Or, one might wear one of those Hagar the Horrible-esque Viking Helmets! A Breastplate and a Long Spear would doubtless be Most Helpful in making your way to the Front of the Line for cocktails (which you will surely be in Dire Need of) during Intermission, as well. Oh, the possibilities are Positively Endless! And, you would, of course, wear your hair in Two Long, Thick, Very Blonde Braids, Dear Reader.

Have a splendid time,
The Etiquette Grrls
(Or, Die Etiquette Mädchen—as long as we're all being Germanic . . .)

Dear Etiquette Grrls,

I will try to atone for the habit of wearing socks with my Birkenstock sandals during the winter months. It does get cold in New England, but I cannot use that as an excuse any longer. Can you suggest an alternative? Mea Culpa.

A Sandals Fan

Dear Sandals,

The Etiquette Grrls are so pleased you've seen the Error of Your Ways, Dear Reader! We remind you that not only is wearing socks with sandals a Terrible Fashion Faux Pas, but also that New England in the Winter is a snowy, rainy place, and dashing about in open-toed shoes is apt to make your socks Rather Damp and

Squishy. And Soggy Socks make for a Nasty Case of Frostbite. For the winter months, the Etiquette Grrls suggest that you purchase at least one pair of Sturdy Oxfords, like Docs, and perhaps a pair of those L.L. Bean Maine Hunting Boots, which are handy footwear for Inclement Weather. Let us know how it works out for you.

Yours truly,
The Etiquette Grrls

Dear Etiquette Grrls,

I've read all of Jane Austen's novels. Does this make me cool?

Nastyboy2000

Dear Nastyboy2000,

Have you also read all of F. Scott Fitzgerald's (or Scott '17, as the Etiquette Grrls like to refer to him) works? Could you have drunk Scott '17 Under the Table? And Held Your Liquor? Now, that might make you cool. But seriously, the Etiquette Grrls remind you that being well-read does not negate the need to be well-mannered at all times.

Regards,
The Etiquette Grrls

CHAPTER FIVE

It's Money, Baby!

O, what Rudeness is perpetrated because of Money! The Etiquette Grrls shudder to think of the flagrant displays of Ostentatious Spending we have witnessed, and the Insipid Whining we have heard from amis whose Wallets were Un Peu Thin. Of course, we do not recommend, Dear Reader, that you Denounce All Currency, revert to a Barter System, and attempt to convince the Sephora Clerk to accept Clamshells in exchange for Urban Decay nailpolish. We all need to deal with money—yet the Etiquette Grrls feel that most people (attention dot-com executives!) could be a Tad more Polite About It.

How Much Cash Should You Carry?

Obviously, you'll need enough money to get yourself home from wherever you are, especially if there is any chance, albeit small, you should become Rather Intoxicated. It is also a good idea to have a bit of cash on hand so that you may buy a yummy brioche should you miss your train and become Faint With Hunger. You will never, *ever* find the Etiquette Grrls without at least twenty dollars in their elegant leather wallets.

It is also very helpful to have several small bills on hand for tipping purposes. It's not cool to ask the Kind Doorman who gets you A Cab to break a Fifty.

However, one can, indeed, carry too much cash. There is probably never any reason for you to have more than one hundred-dollar bill on your person at any given time, unless you are a Drug Dealer. Making big purchases is what Credit Cards are for.

The New Fifties, Twenties, Tens, and Fives

Ugly, ugly, ugly. The Etiquette Grrls like that these bills are still crisp, but, let's face it, none of the men on U.S. money is really attractive enough to be enlarged. (Should our bills have depicted, say, Robert Sean Leonard, this might have been acceptable, but Andrew Jackson was a bitter man and this shows in his ugly little mouth.) It is rather rude of the U.S. Treasury not to have consulted the Etiquette Grrls before altering the appearance of our Legal Tender. The Etiquette Grrls don't think much of Messing With Tradition Just for the Sake of Messing With It, and after all, Is anything More Traditional than American Greenbacks? After all, they are printed on Crane's Paper, one of the Etiquette Grrls' Very Favorite Things! If we really *had* to Redesign Our Currency, why couldn't we make it Pretty, like the darling old French Francs?

Which Credit Card You Should Have

People with Too Much Time on Their Hands frequently spend hours, if not days, researching Annual Fees, Lines of Credit, Grace Periods, etc., before choosing a credit card. This pales in comparison with the Etiquette Grrls' chief concerns—what kind of card is it, where can you use it, and, most importantly, is it pretty?

First, you are only allowed to have a Visa or MasterCard as your general credit card. Discover, Diners Club, etc., are Not Cool. (What are you planning to "Discover" with the piddly two cents you get back at the end of the year? And you can bet that any restaurant the Etiquette Grrls would dine at would, frankly, decline to be part of some "Club.") You are also, of course, allowed to have Charge Plates for major department stores such as Lord & Taylor, Nordstrom, etc.

You should not, under any circumstances, hold a credit card bearing a picture of Your Alma Mater, (or, horrors, Your Actual Mater), several fluffy kittens, or a Pop Group. Tasteful people, such as the Etiquette Grrls, carry plain Platinum Visas, which offer a rather crazy amount of credit and, more importantly, are a muted metallic silver, which looks quite fetching in a black wallet. Should you not have as good credit as the Etiquette Grrls, then, for goodness' sake, obtain a regular, navy blue Visa and hide it behind something else. American Express looks civil enough, but, according to the mom of one of the Etiquette Grrls, "Their people are surly," and, well, when an Etiquette Mom feels that way, the Etiquette Grrls don't need to hear any more.

Visiting the ATM

The Etiquette Grrls just love that we are able to get our hands on Cold, Hard Cash at any time of the day or night. After all, a Girl just never knows when she's going to be overcome avec hunger, and need to stop for a light déjeuner, or when she's going to have the opportunity to Knock Back a Few dans a Swanky Bar. But what rudeness one is apt to encounter at the ATM, Dear Reader! Shocking! As if it weren't enough that All Banks seemingly have un petit problem keeping Their Machines stocked avec money, must we be subjected to Rude Behavior on top of it all? Herewith, the Etiquette Grrls' Official List of Things You Need To Be Told whilst in line at the Automatic Teller Machine.

- **Make It Snappy.** People in line at the ATM just need twenty bucks for lunch, dammit, and there's no reason why anyone should have to stand outside in the Freezing Cold for an Hour to get it. If you are making so many Complex Transactions that it appears you are attempting to Overtake A Small Country, then the Etiquette Grrls feel that you should either wait until the queue has lessened, or let people who just have One Quick Thing go ahead of you. Or, you might do something Really Retro, and actually go *inside* the Bank, where the Etiquette Grrls have heard they have Nice People who will assist you.

- **Form a Nice, Orderly Queue.** Egads, the Etiquette Grrls loathe Disorder! However, do not allow the Nice, Orderly Queue to Block the Sidewalk Entirely, as this prevents the flow of Pedestrian Traffic, and it is Very Rude to force Poor Pedestrians to Walk In The Dangerous Street in order to skirt around a Belligerent and Immobile Mob.

- **Give the person at the ATM some Elbow Room.** There's nothing worse than the feeling that someone is Breathing Down Your Neck. Especially when you are banking.

- **Don't toss your receipts on the ground.** Throw them out, or better yet, save them to record in Your Checkbook. (Don't you want to know at a Glance if you have Ample Funds to buy that Cashmere Twin Set/take that trip to Florence/take the bus home?)

- **Don't forget to take Your Card back.**

- **If you find Somebody Else's Card, don't Steal It.** Turn it into the bank immédiatement, or 'phone the number on the back of the card and report its AWOL Status!

How to Carry Your Cash

The Etiquette Grrls recommend that you use a small wallet made of Real Leather in a neutral color (e.g., black). You do not need to carry a photograph of everyone you've ever met; you do not need to carry enough change to while away quelques heures dans le Casino. You also should Make A Habit of removing the myriad Banana Republic receipts from your wallet on, say, a weekly basis.

Your wallet should not weigh more than your Small Pet. (And, for heaven's sake, your Small Pet should not be kept in your wallet. This is not good.)

The Etiquette Grrls are exceedingly Not Fond of People Who Think Huge, Heavy Leather Agendas Are The Same Thing As Wallets. (We have no problem with small, tasteful datebooks; however, hefty, nylon "agenda books" can See Us In Hell. If you fancy lugging around a heavy notebook with a Velcro closure, we suggest you go back to fifth grade and acquire a Trapper Keeper. Perhaps the one with Smurfs.) It is usually our experience that the most interesting, busy people we meet are *not* the ones carrying around the Giant Planners. In fact, the people carrying the Giant Planners are usually Management Consultants, who are as intrinsically interesting as, say, Lawn Chairs.

FLAUNTING ONE'S WEALTH

It is truly an excellent thing to be Wealthy, yet, the Etiquette Grrls admit, it is complicated. When we say "Wealthy," we mean Really Loaded—and, what with the cybercommerce boom, there are an awful lot of new, young, Filthy Rich Folk running around who have absolutely no idea how they should act.

First of all, if one has acquired what is known as "New Money," one should immediately play down its newness. It is most uncool to run around exclaiming with glee over how much your net worth increases every hour. It is equally uncool to buy every newfangled item one encounters—the Etiquette Grrls have Great Disdain for anyone (Mr. Gates, this means you) who would decorate their home with giant hi-res LCDs when they can obviously afford Real Paintings by people like Sargent. One's house should be as comfortable, exquisitely furnished, and well-equipped as one can afford, but under no circumstances should you be able to give it Voice Commands. Nor should you employ Wee Housekeeping Robots in lieu of Real Servants. You should not live like the Jetsons.

However, if you are wealthy, everyone will know it, and you

will have special responsibilities. Cheapness in known Rich People is THOR. You should not be whipping out a calculator to split the tab; nor should you give presents like Russell Stover candies when you can clearly afford to buy tasteful gifts at Tiffany's or order yummy food baskets from Zingerman's. You should take extra care to avoid whining about how broke you are if you are a Trust-Fund Baby.

Actually, the Etiquette Grrls aren't sure anyone should ever discuss how broke she is, or, conversely, how loaded she is. Either everyone knows this already, or you are lying, or you have been either the Perpetrator or the Victim of a crime. In the latter case, perhaps a brief discussion is appropriate:

Emma: I'm sorry, but might we grab a croissant for lunch instead of keeping our reservation at Lahiere's? I've just been mugged, and have neither Cash nor Credit Cards.

(Note that Emma (1) apologizes; (2) suggests a tasty alternative to the planned pricey lunch; (3) explains fully.)
The appropriate response is, of course:

Katharine: You poor dear! Are you certain you're all right? (Emma nods yes.) Well, then I think there is even more occasion to go to Lahiere's, as there is A Very Good Bar, and anyone who has been mugged obviously needs A Good, Strong Drink. My treat. How awful! (etc.)

Otherwise, however, it's best to keep all discussion of money to one's self. Should you receive a Raise, or embark upon A Very Good Career, good for you—now shut up. It is not cool, if you are, say, a second-year law student, to sit down with your Struggling Writer Friend and figure out that your summer job will pay you more than she earns in a year. Your Noble Writer Friend probably already has some idea that Corporate Tools make rather more than she, and, surely, she is too cool to be hanging around with a sellout such as you; most likely, she will have a great opportunity to mock you in print, and you will then be sorry for the rest of Your Nasty Little Life. Not that this has happened to the Etiquette Grrls, or anything.

NOBLESSE OBLIGE

It is a great faux pas to have money and use it poorly. It is not really obligatory for you to spend all your money foolishly, but it is in Extremely Poor Taste to have Heaps of Cash and not enjoy it. Obviously, you will want to have tasteful, elegant parties in your home for groups of Your Close Friends. However, Dear Reader, how can you tell what is Acceptable, Nay, Expected of You, and what is Tacky and Overdone? Let's compare.

GOOD	BAD
· Sending a Lovely Arrangement of out-of-season flowers to an acquaintance who is Ailing.	· Having a greenhouse installed in Said Acquaintance's backyard as a "surprise."
· Hosting a weekend party for Your Closest Friends at Your Ancestral Country Home, complete with Excellent Cuisine and Plentiful Liquor.	· Having Eminem play a private concert during it.
· You and your best friend have always talked about going to Italy and France after graduation. Your Trust Fund kicks in while you're abroad. You still backpack most of the way, but for your last week in Rome, you splurge on a Suite in a Former Palazzo for you and your friend.	· You're 24. You go on vacation and bring your Personal Assistant and your Trainer.

• A matched set of Beautiful Leather Luggage.	• FedExing one's bags from one's home to one's hotel.
• Beautifully tailored, understated suits.	• The matching designer-logo suit/ stockings/shoes/barrette/bag look. Please, show some imagination.
• Wearing your Mom's Pearls in your passport photo.	• Having your Passport Photo airbrushed.

Tipping

Why does one tip? Because, Kats and Kittens, nearly every nice thing in life depends upon it! Imagine, Dear Reader, a world in which we always Ate Meals We Prepared at Home, Toted Our Own Heavy Valises Everywhere, and, horror of horrors, Cut and Colored Our Own Hair—without exception, everyone would be Miserable, Exhausted, and Terribly Coiffed. Thankfully, there are People Whose Job It Is to handle such things. And, out of respect for them and gratitude for the Services They Render, you must know how to tip them properly. For example, if you've just moved to a Nice Apartment in The Big City, you may be unaware that you're supposed to tip Your Super and Your Doorman. Fear not; the Etiquette Grrls are here to assist!

However, there's more to tipping than knowing whom to tip and what percentage gratuity you should leave. There is such a thing as tipping with grace, and the Etiquette Grrls can help you become An Expert. When you know you'll be in a situation that requires tipping, try to have cash available in the right size bills. It is embarrassing to ask the Pizza Guy to break a fifty, or to leave a Tower of Quarters on the table at a Fancy Restaurant. Furthermore, it is Bad Manners to figure out a tip to the Very Last Cent. While the Etiquette Grrls realize that some people really enjoy figuring out 15 percent of $61.85, we think it looks a little Cheap. Simply estimate, and always round up; a nice, even $10 would be good. Also, when you have lunch alone, and only order a bowl of soup, and the standard 15 to 20 percent tip of your bill equals forty-seven cents, you *must* leave at least a dollar. This applies to all sorts of tips, from restaurants, to salons, to taxi-cabs.

Lastly, remember: Tipping is only about the exact service provided. It is not the Flower Delivery Boy's fault that your Idiot Ex-Boyfriend sent you a bouquet, so, although you don't want it, you should still tip the Delivery Boy who lugged it to your Fifth-Floor Apartment. People whose income depends upon gratuities shouldn't suffer due to Your Personal Issues.

RESTAURANTS

The standard restaurant tip in the United States is 15 to 20 percent. In some states, you can calculate this by simply tripling the tax shown on the bill. The Etiquette Grrls love these states, as they help us Avoid Math! However, Tip Math isn't all that painful . . . just chop the last number off the total and move the decimal point over one digit to the left (thus giving you 10 percent of the bill). You then have a Starting Point upon which to base your tip, and can figure 15 percent, 20 percent, etc. from there. Dear Reader, practice this, even if Math makes you Break Out in Hives. If your Waiter has been especially Accommodating, you should leave something in excess of 15 to 20 percent to express Your Appreciation. If you are in a large party, sometimes a gratuity will be added automatically. Check the menu when you are seated, or the Bill when it arrives.

If your check comes in a Leather(ette) Folder, leave the tip in it—either with the money to cover the check, or after the Waiter has returned with your change. In a Diner, where you pay the Cashier, stack tip money neatly on the table. If you pay by credit card, just add the amount of the tip on the appropriate line.

Finally, if service was bad, tip less, or do not tip at all, but do not express dissatisfaction by leaving thirteen cents in a water glass or writing a curse word in ketchup on a dollar bill. The Etiquette

Grrls find this *so* childish and boorish! Your dissatisfaction would be more graciously expressed with a Simple, Quick, Stern Word avec the Manager.

BARS

Always be generous to Bartenders and/or Barmaids, or you'll get Watery Drinks. (And the Etiquette Grrls *despise* Watery Drinks, we'll have you know.) If you have a tab, tip the Bartender 15 percent of it; handle it as you would a restaurant check. If you fetch individual drinks, tip about the same percentage when you pay, but never less than about one dollar per drink. If the bartender says, "That'll be five dollars," you should hand him six dollars. If, at a Bar, you get Table Service, you tip as outlined above under restaurants. In this case, do not also tip the bartender. That would be too much largesse. Not, of course, that the Etiquette Grrls are against Being Generous—nay, we're All For Generosity, but one doesn't ever want to be accused of Flaunting One's Wealth!

SALONS

At a Beauty Salon or Spa, you tip everyone who touches you. People who perform major services, like haircuts or facials, get 10 to 15 percent of the cost of that service. (This means that if you have several things done in one trip, you should ask for a price list so you can tip appropriately.) If an Underling gives you a shampoo, tip the Underling a few dollars. Good salons have Tiny Tip Envelopes at the reception desk. You put tip money in one of these, seal it, and write "For Jane Stylist, From Priscilla Winterthorpe." Leave it for the receptionist to deliver. You may also leave tip money at the stylists' stations, but the Etiquette Grrls prefer the envelope method. It is vexing to worry about Doling Out Tips while one's Hair is Dripping, or, when one has finished, to Retrace One's Path through the salon, hoping to find the right stations. And, unless a stylist sees you leave the money, she might not know it's from you!

One exception to these rules: If the Salon Owner tends to you, do not tip her.

MOVERS

When you move, you are at the Movers' Mercy, and you must *never* imply you're not going to tip! Otherwise, you might find your china in shards, and your sofa mysteriously Gone Missing. At the completion of Your Move, if everything arrives safely, you tip both the Head Mover and his Assistants—about twenty-five to fifty dollars to The Guy In Charge, and fifteen to thirty dollars to each of his crew members, depending on the size of Your Move and the amount of care which was taken with Your Belongings. If the Movers did any of your packing for you, you might tip them A Bit More. And of course, should you be moving into or out of a fifth-floor walk-up, or it's 110 degrees in the Shade, you should up the tips accordingly as well. Also, Dear Reader, you should not give the Head Mover a Lump Sum, and depend on him to divvy it up fairly among His Crew. First of all, he may not be Trustworthy, and secondly (and More Importantly), it is *much* more gracious to give each of the Crew Members their tip in person, with a Word of Thanks for all their Hard Work. Finally, if there are Different Teams of Movers on Each End (common in long-distance moves), tip the First Team when they are dismissed. (Just the Assistants; the Head Mover will be staying with Your Stuff, and you'll see him at Your Final Destination. One hopes.) You would then, of course, tip the Second Team at your destination.

DELIVERIES

It would be a drag if, every time a Beau sent flowers, one had to drive to the Florist's and lug a big arrangement back to one's flat! The Flower Delivery Boy gets a few dollars for his trouble.

For Food Delivery, tip 10 to 15 percent of the bill. Don't figure this out to the last cent—just estimate and round up.

The Pizza Boy should be tipped at least one dollar per pizza, plus whatever Odd Change is left over. If he does Something Extraordinary, such as delivering Your Pizza promptly and without telephoning for Directions, even though the address on the delivery slip was incorrect, you should be a Bit More Generous, to award his Astuteness. (This, Dear Reader, amazingly, has actually happened to the Etiquette Grrls! Their Favorite Pizza Joint's Delivery Boys are Pretty Swift on the Uptake!)

CABS
Generally 15 to 20 percent of the Fare, but never less than a dollar. If the cabbie is Unforgivably Surly, or Threatening, or Fails To Take You Where You Asked To Go, you should feel free to adjust the tip accordingly.

PORTERS
These days, Dear Reader, the Etiquette Grrls think it's pretty unlikely you'll even have the opportunity to tip an airport or railroad porter (also known as "skycaps" and "redcaps," respectively), because the EGs can't quite say when we last saw one. Nevertheless, we hear they exist, and perhaps you will find yourself in some Remote City where they are Plentiful. In which case, they are tipped in manner similar to Hotel Bellhops (see below). However, in some Airports and Railroad Stations, Porters have a Fixed Fee of one dollar per bag. In such an instance, you should then tip the fellow a dollar or two extra (because he has to Fork Over a percentage of his fixed-rate earnings to Somebody Else.) One does not tip Flight Attendants, Pilots, Bus Drivers, or Railroad Conductors, no matter how grateful you are that you survived Your Trip without getting into A Terrible Accident.

HOTELS
Lately, it seems like A Real Hotel is pretty hard to come by. Sadly, Dear Reader, it's more likely that you'll being staying in a Holiday

Inn, where you'll have to lug your own damn suitcase up to your room, and the closest thing to Room Service is a Pizza Hut across the street. But maybe someday you'll find yourself at a good, old-fashioned Full-Service Hotel, and in that case, you'll have Lots of People to Tip. Here are the Biggies:

Doormen: Naturally, one does not tip the Doorman every time one walks through the door. But if he assists you and Your Luggage in or out of your car, you should give him a dollar or two. If you ask the Doorman to get you a Taxi, you should again give him at least a dollar, and even three or four dollars if he puts himself At Risk, such as by standing outside in A Driving Blizzard, or if he is inadvertently Mown Down by the Speeding Taxi he hailed for you.

Bellhops: If a Bellhop carries your luggage to or from Your Room, you should give him one dollar per bag, but not less than two dollars. You still must tip him, even if he does not actually carry Your Bags, burro-fashion, but uses one of those Wheelie Things.

The Maid: You should leave at least two dollars per day, and more if the Maid has done anything Special for you, like fetch you extra blankets. You should leave her tip on the desk in an envelope marked "Housekeeping" at the end of your stay. Better yet, if you see her in the Hall, it's nice to give it to her in person, with a kind Word of Thanks.

Room Service: Often, in Nice Hotels, it will say on the Room Service Menu that a Gratuity is added to your Total Bill (in addition to a Room Service Fee), and this, of course, is a Tip. If the Gratuity is not included, you should tip The Waiter at least 15 percent of your bill, but never less than two dollars, even if he only brought you Tonic Water for your Gin.

PEOPLE IN AND AROUND YOUR APARTMENT BUILDING

The Etiquette Grrls are fortunate enough to live in a very-nice-but-not-extravagant Apartment Building in a relatively posh part of town. Lucky us, we know, but even so, Dear Reader, we don't have a Staff in our building, and we know it's going to be a Cold Day In Hell before the Landlord sends anyone around to take a look at that big hunk of the Dining Room Ceiling that just fell down. But maybe you, Dear Reader, are fortunate enough to have a live-in Super, and perhaps you even live in a "Doorman Building." Superb! Well Done, Dear Reader! If you do live in a building avec A Staff, it's customary to give the folks who help carry your Groceries, keep the Riff-Raff at bay, sign for Packages while you're Out, and in short, make your day A Bit Easier, A Little Something. Generally this is done at Christmastime, but you may tip throughout the year if you'd prefer, and then give a Smidgie Bit Less for The Christmas Tip. The amount you give to the People In Your Building of course depends on Many Things—the part of the Country in which you live, the Luxuriousness of Your Building, the Helpfulness of The Staff, and so on. But, the Etiquette Grrls would recommend about fifty dollars annually for the Super, and thirty-five dollars for the Doorman—bearing in mind, Dear Reader, that these amounts could be doubled in a Very Good Building in an Expensive City, like New York.

THE POSTMAN

Once Upon a Time, Dear Reader, when the Etiquette Grrls' Parents were Young Whippersnappers, it was expected to give The Mailman, who made his Rounds Through Rain, Sleet, And Other Nasty Things, a Healthy Bonus at Christmas, and perhaps a nice cup of Hot Cocoa or Coffee. And well, in fact, the EGs remember that this was so even when they were Growing Up. But now the Dear Old U.S.P.S. is run like A Private Business, and the Mailmen are paid Rather Well. And we're told that they're not *allowed* to Take

Tips. However, the Etiquette Grrls remind their Dear Readers that they should always make an effort to Become Friends with The Postman, who really is a Good Person to know . . . not just so all your Mail gets to you in One Piece, but often he can tell you All Sorts of Interesting and Informative Things about Your Neighborhood and the People In It! You should, of course, always have a Kind Word for Mr. Postman when you see him, and also remember to thank him if he brings a package up to your door rather than leaving it in The Lobby, or some other such Nicety.

OTHER PEOPLE YOU DON'T TIP

You know, Dear Reader, it's not that the EGs don't have An Immense Amount of Sympathy for Those Earning Minimum Wage, but it seems pretty silly that these days, wherever you go—Starbucks, the Corner Deli, the Seafood Counter at the Supermarket, the counter at the Mini-Mart—everywhere, in short—there's a Can sitting on the counter bearing a Magic Markered label reading "TIPS." Now, if you're sitting at the Counter at Joe's Diner and the waitress brings you a cup of Tomato Soup, then yes, of course you would tip her. But at the Deli, where as you stand at the cash register, some kid flings a mayonnaise-stained paper bag containing your Chicken Salad sandwich at you? Well, no. Now of course, Dear Reader, if you go to Pumpernickel's Deli every single blessed day for lunch, and the staff is always cheerful, pleasant, and helpful, and they're always giving you things On The House, then sure, feel free to toss a buck or two into The Pot. Perhaps instead of dropping in a quarter every day or so, you could give a somewhat more generous amount once a month or every couple of weeks. And especially at Christmastime, you could throw something a little extra their way. But it's not absolutely required. The General Rule of Thumb: If you have Table or Counter Service, you tip as you would in any restaurant. Self-Serve and To-Go items, there's no need to.

This should be Blatantly Obvious, but one does not tip someone who provides you with a Medical Service. This gets a bit tricky, but the EGs trust, Dear Reader, that you will get the swing of things. A Chemical Peel performed by a Dermatologist in His Office=No Tip. Some much milder (we hope) form of a Chemical Peel performed by an Aesthetician at Your Local Day Spa=Tip. Deep-tissue massage performed by a Licensed Massage Therapist in a Physical Therapy Clinic=No Tip. Hot Stone Massage in Your Local Day Spa=Tip. Got it, Dear Reader?

Please, for the Love of God, don't even *think* about tipping Your Professors, or the Hostess of a Dinner Party you attend, or the Judge who's hearing your case in Traffic Court, or a Chivalric Boy who holds a door for you! In all cases like this, offering a tip is Wildly Insulting, and may even be Interpreted as An Attempted Bribe.

Now, remember, Dear Reader, these are just a Few General Tipping Guidelines that the Etiquette Grrls have laid out for you— there are many things you have to take into consideration when figuring tips—the part of the country you're in, the swankiness of the establishment, and of course, the quality of service provided. As with most things, Dear Reader, the Etiquette Grrls urge you to use Your Best Judgment. And when in doubt, err to the side of Generosity. Being a Cheapskate never got anyone anywhere, Dear Reader! Which is not to say that if The Service is Abysmal, you shouldn't adjust the tip accordingly and Complain to The Management. But there's no need to get Tyrannical and Withhold a Tip if your Poor Beleaguered Waitress accidentally brought you a Sprite instead of a Coke—remember that everyone has A Bad Day every now and again. Most importantly, remember you must always be courteous and pleasant to those who are providing you with a Service—The Biggest Tip in the World will never compensate for Rude and Unpleasant Behavior on your part!

Questions and Answers on Various and Sundry

Dear Etiquette Grrls,

As we all know, when one inhabits an apartment building, it is quite an ordeal to do one's laundry. In fact, it can even turn into a life-threatening Game of Skill. I have enjoyed many a round of "Find the Melted Crayon" and "Spot the Bleach Leak" initiated by other inhabitants of my wee dwelling.

However, one game that I do not like at all is "Washer-Dryer Tailgating"—you know, when you are doing your numerous loads of laundry and someone else decides to place his or her full laundry basket on top of the machine, thus "claiming" it for the next cycle. Clearly, if you see someone else's laundry stuff already in the room, and there's still a load or two to go, you should not assume that you can just sneak on in there and interrupt the process! Now, there is only one washer and one dryer in my building, and I can understand that time is of the essence for other inhabitants, but recently, a visiting friend of one of my neighbors decided to play this Wretched Tailgating Game. What should I do, dear Etiquette Grrls? Is it rude to say something to this Visitor? I mean, after all, I pay to live there—and he doesn't. Shouldn't I have dibs if I have already started to do my washing? Any advice on how to resolve this matter would be most appreciated, especially since this person has recently become a Repeat Offender.

Sincerely,
Sit-and-Spin-Cycle Sister of Etiquette

Dear Sit-and-Spin-Cycle,

Oh, yes, Dear Reader, Laundry Chores are the Bane of the Etiquette Grrls' Existence! We really must look into acquiring A Laundress one of these days. The Etiquette Grrls are quite familiar with this "Washer-Dryer Tailgating" game of which you speak—the people who initiate this game are the same sort who think it's très amusant to take Your Laundry out of the dryer before it is Fully Dry, and dump it unceremoniously upon the Filthy Floor. It goes without saying that this is Disgraceful Behavior, Dear Reader! And when People Who Do Not Live In Your Building partake in such behavior? Horrors! You are right, Dear Reader, and you should have preference over a Laundry Room Squatter. It may be tedious for some, but Laundry Rooms are first come, first served, and one should be able to finish one's laundry in peace. That's just the way it is. Perhaps you could inquire of the Visitor (avec a very Innocent Demeanor, of course) if the Laundry Facilities in his own building are Out of Order? You should offer your regrets, and provide him with the name and address of a nearby Laundromat. If this fails to riddle the Offending Party with Unbearable Guilt, you might have to Give Him a Taste of His Own Medicine. (Not that, generally speaking, the Etiquette Grrls approve of Playing Dirty, of course.) But you could, if worse comes to worst, loiter around until the opportunity avails itself to you, and intercept his laundry. One hopes that the Tailgater will Get the Message.

Happy Laundering,
The Etiquette Grrls

Dear Etiquette Grrls,

I don't really care for my roommate too much. Frankly, she frightens me. Also, she's kind of mean to me. She flat-out refuses to give me my phone messages; she ate all the cookies my Mom put in the last Care Package she sent me; she sometimes throws all my stuff out in the hallway while I'm gone; she also sleepwalks, and is much too fond of this Voodoo Doll she has. Once, she had the locks changed when I went 'round to the Common Room for a few minutes. I've talked to my R.A. and I can't change rooms. I've tried being nice, and it just makes her even more difficult. What should I do? I don't want to sink to her level and be rude or mean.

College Freshman

Dear Freshman,

Sounds like you need to Scare Her Off. You could throw a Threatening Look her way now and again to set the stage. Then, have one of your Dear Friends call and leave a message for you (assuming you share an answering machine or a voice mailbox) saying something to the effect of, "I'm calling for Miss Priscilla Mullins. Miss Mullins, this is Agent John Alden from the F.B.I. I'm calling to let you know that you have the go-ahead on The Plan. All systems are go. We'll be in touch when the Mission is accomplished." Make sure your roommate hears the message, and if she should ask you what it means, look mysterious and say nothing. If pressed, tell her that you "really can't say." Now, while this is not a Direct Threat (which is not only rude, but could get you in trouble with your school's administration), it should be mysterious enough to put the Fear of The Lord into her.

Very truly yours,
The Etiquette Grrls

Dear Etiquette Grrls,

How do you kick someone out of your house when he or she is visiting?

Sincerely,
Frazzled Hostess

Dear Frazzled Hostess,

While the Etiquette Grrls have always said that entertaining can be a practically hallucinogenic lot of fun, it's horrid indeed when a guest outstays his or her welcome. How Rude! It is particularly annoying when Your Houseguest begins to resemble A Squatter, but regular (i.e., non-overnight) guests who linger are vexing as well.

When inviting a Houseguest to stay Chez Toi, be sure to specify when the visit needs to end. You might say, "I'd love to see you for a long weekend! What are you doing the last week in July? If you're free, maybe you could come to Osterville on Thursday evening and stay through Sunday. I have to go on a business trip that Monday but it'd be great to see you for the weekend!" If the guest mentions sticking around for An Extra Day, simply remind him or her of your Other Engagements. If the guest is not a Horrible Boor (and if the guest is, maybe he or she shouldn't be visiting you), he or she will Take The Hint.

As for your guests at any Soirée you might happen to throw, if you've provided alcohol, and if your friends are anything like the Etiquette Grrls', you may very well have Drunken Stragglers at the end of the evening. The Etiquette Grrls feel that unless A Cab is An Option, you simply have to put up with the Tipsy Folk until they Sober Up, or offer them Your Couch.

And then, there's also the Following Scenario: You invite Your Friend over for a cup of tea after the late screening of *The Talented Mr. Ripley*, but suddenly, it's 4 A.M., your supply of Fortnum & Mason Darjeeling is depleted, and Your Friend isn't budging from your lovely settee. The Etiquette Grrls suggest the following series of Subtle Hints: (1) Yawn. (2) Mention The Time. (3) Remark that gee, you've finished all the tea. (4) Suddenly remember The Very Important Breakfast Meeting You Have With the CEO in Just Three and a Half Hours. (5) Fit of yawning. (6) Collect cups and tea paraphernalia; put away. (7) Go and get into Your PJ's and Bunny Slippers; brush your teeth; start going through the rest of Your Nighttime Routine (i.e., curlers, clay masques, etc.). (8) Fall Dead Asleep at table. Or . . . you might try simply saying, "What a lovely film, despite Vapid Gwyneth and Smirky Matt, and it was smashing to have a Good Chat with you! I'm tired as anything, though, and I've got to go to work early tomorrow, er, this morning! Why don't we have lunch next week?" Unless Your Friend is totally Bereft of Reason, this surely will send her On Her Merry Way.

However, Dear Reader, remember that it is Not Kind to Shoo Someone Out Into The Cold if he or she is having An Emergency. If Your Best Friend showed up on Your Doorstep in Crisis Mode, then, well, it's Your Responsibility as a Dear Friend to sit up with her and listen to her rant, cry, or what-have-you, and provide some Moral Support and Hot Tea, even if that means you don't get any sleep yourself. You would, after all, expect Nothing Less if the roles were reversed, would you not, Dear Reader? What it comes down to, Dear Reader, is knowing when to Be Firm, and When To Be A Friend.

Cheers,
The Etiquette Grrls

Dear Etiquette Grrls,

I'm always up at The Crack of Dawn. How early may I place a telephone call to a Private Residence on a weekend? What if I'm calling a friend?

In a 'Phoning Frenzy

Dear 'Phoning Frenzy,

Well, the Etiquette Grrls themselves are most definitely not Morning People, Dear Reader. Even if we are, technically speaking, awake before The Crack of Noon on weekends, we're generally A Wee Bit Groggy before we've enjoyed A Good Brunch, perused The *Times*, and maybe watched a bit of Television. And a Groggy Etiquette Grrl is a Grumpy Etiquette Grrl! We think that a lot of people enjoy some Peace and Quiet on weekends, Dear Reader, so we'd not recommend calling anybody before, say, the early part of Lunchtime.

Now, Dear Reader, if you know for An Absolute Fact that the person who you are calling has been up and about for hours and hours, and has already walked the dog, done the dusting, and whipped up a loaf or three of Cranberry Bread from scratch all before 7 A.M., then sure, go ahead and place your call. As long as you are Positively Positive that you will not disturb or awaken anyone else in the Household.

The Etiquette Grrls are just wondering, Dear Reader—whom are you planning to call at home on the Weekends who's Not A Friend? One would follow the same rules for calling Relations as one would for Dear Friends, and besides, the Etiquette Grrls trust that you are aware of the Morning Routine of, say, Your Parents, Dear Reader.

Yours very truly,
The Etiquette Grrls

CHAPTER SIX

Gifts and Greediness

Thank Heavens for Tiffany's Catalogue!: The Gifts You Should Be Giving

The Etiquette Grrls know that everyone adores both Giving and Receiving Presents! But how does one select a gift for Your Loved One from the Staggering Array of items available for purchase? Well, Dear Reader, there are, of course, some stores where practically everything in stock is Just Lovely—for instance, we all know that Good Jewelry comes in those Wee Blue Boxes from Holly Golightly's Favorite Store. But Big-Ticket Items don't always make the Best Gifts, Dear Reader. The trick is to think about what the recipient would really, truly like, and maybe that's just a Little Inexpensive Something, such as say, a book or CD or some such. Also, if you happen, Dear Reader, to be blessed avec a Wee Artistic Streak, it's often quite nice if you Make Something Yourself. For example, hand-knit Argyle Socks might make a Smashing Christmas Present for Your Favorite Boy! Trust us, Dear Reader—as much as the Etiquette Grrls adore things like Good Jewelry, we'd rather receive a Small and Thoughtful Gift than some Pricey Gee-Gaw that was Blindly Selected from A Catalogue.

Further—and the Etiquette Grrls would hope that we wouldn't

even need to point this out to you, Dear Reader—one does not give a gift expecting anything in return. It fills the Etiquette Grrls with delight when we're out and about, and we suddenly stumble across A Little Something that we know one of our Dear Friends would adore! And then to find just the right wrapping paper and ribbons! Oh, Dear Reader, it makes the Etiquette Grrls Giddy avec Happiness! One gives gifts out of the Goodness of One's Heart—because you, Dear Reader, want to. The joy, Dear Reader, is truly in the giving, as corny as that may sound to jaded, Post-Post-Modern Ears. But honestly, the Etiquette Grrls don't want your Insincere Presents, thank you very much.

Occasions That Do and Do Not Merit a Gift

YOUR BEST FRIEND'S BIRTHDAY

The EGs think you should give a Wee Something to a Good Friend to show you remember his or her birthday. (Now, Dear Reader, you do know Your Good Friends' Birthdays, do you not? Of course you do. Should you find yourself prone to Wee Memory Lapses—as are we all, upon occasion—you should write down all your Dear Friends' Birthdays on Your New Calendar every year, just as a Wee Reminder to yourself.) As with all presents, a Birthday Gift for a Friend need not be Expensive or Elaborate—it should simply show that you took Special Care in selecting a present that Your Good Friend will really love. This is not a Difficult Task; it simply requires a bit of Advance Planning and Creative Thought. Remember, it would be Rather Insulting for you to give your friend something she already owns, which is On Prominent Display in her apartment, and which you surely would have noticed in the umpteen times you've been to her flat. It would also be THOR to purchase something for her which you, as Her Good Friend, really should know she will have No Use For, such as a Bicycle Lock when your friend does not own a Bicycle. Also, please do not select some sort of prepackaged, generic gift thingamabob, like a Plastic Frame saying

"Happy Birthday to My Friend"—this only shows that you didn't Think in Advance about Her Birthday and resorted to picking up the first thing you saw in the Card Shop. For this reason, the EGs do not feel it is appropriate for us to Suggest Particular Gifts for this person, as we regret that we have not had the pleasure of Getting to Know Your Good Friends. We can, however, give you a list of the Kinds of Things we've given Our Good Friends, so you can see how we go about selecting them.

- Vintage Books on subjects Dear to Our Friends' Hearts. The EGs, for example, collect Vintage Etiquette Books, and adore finding Rare Copies for each other! If you know someone's Favorite Author, you can easily find a nice edition of one of his or her works. Sometimes you might find an edition in Another Language, which can be Highly Amusing if your friend can read it in the translation! (In particular. the EGs recommend German Editions of books by Scott '17. *Zärlicht ist die Nacht!*)

- Vintage Accessories for Their Home. Now, we wouldn't advise giving a Delicately Embroidered Linen Tablecloth to a Young Bachelor sharing a flat with Five Other Young Gentlemen who only use their Dining Room as a place to stack up their Beer Cans, but you get the idea. Visit a few Antique Shops and browse. You just might find something perfect, like an Old Sign that says, in large bronze letters, "SHAMELESS CAD"! The EGs actually once saw such a sign in Lambertville, New Jersey, and to This Very Day, regret not purchasing it! (Incidentally, this leads us to one of the EGs' Cardinal Rules of Shopping: When you see Something You Like, and you can Afford It, Buy It. Because it won't be there when you Come Back.)

- Something We've Witnessed Our Friend Admire. Have you taken a Shopping Trip with a friend, and witnessed him Pining

Over a particular objet d'art? It would be Simply Grand of you to return to the store (sans Your Friend, of course), and pick up that item, even if His Next Birthday is Eleven Months Away. (Just be sure to remember where you put it, Dear Reader. Such things have a way of Going AWOL in One's Closet!) Failing that, make a note of what your friend admired, and when you embark on a search for a gift for Your Friend, see if you can find something similar. Few of us can afford Authentic Tiffany Vases, Dear Reader, but you might find a Gorgeous Coffee-Table Book on Tiffany Vases that Your Friend would adore.

- Something You've Created Yourself. Maybe you're a Talented Artist, and you could paint a Beautiful Watercolor for Your Friend. Maybe you're a Gifted Baker, and can make the most Heavenly Brownies Imaginable. Your Dear Friends will love to receive something you made especially for them! (We would say, however, that Having a Special Talent doesn't excuse you from your obligation of giving a present Your Friend will actually like. You may be a Skilled Tattoo Artist, but your Un-Inked Friend will most likely not be too keen on Your Offer to cover her back with a giant image of Mount Rushmore. And if you're a Baker, make sure you don't prepare Almond Macaroons for someone who Can't Abide Almonds, even if they're Your Latest Specialty. Capisce?)

- Something They'd Wholeheartedly Love, But Wouldn't Buy For Themselves. Whether that's a Silly Toy from Their Childhood someone always coveted but Never Owned (eBay is terrific for finding such things), or Little Luxurious Items (e.g., Powder and Bath Salts in the scent they normally wear, if they only currently have The Perfume; a Reading Rack for the Tub; or, for an Avid Gardener, Really Top-of-the-Line Hand Tools), we're sure you can find something that's Just Perfect.

TMAS/HANUKKAH/KWANZAA/THE WINTER SOLSTICE

never of these December Events you celebrate, chances are, you'll be Exchanging Gifts with Certain People. Immediate Family and Close Friends come to mind—follow the advice we just gave for a Close Friend's Birthday Gift. But what about Your Secretary, or the Superintendent of Your Building, or Your Dog Walker? For some of these people, a Nice Tip is Expected—we've covered that in our section about Tipping (pages 137–145). But under no circumstances should you tip someone who Works For You!! Your Company may have a Holiday Bonus Program, which is, of course, Peachy Keen, but still, if someone who Assists You has done a Splendid Job, a Personally Selected Present might be in order at the Holidays. Of course, you should Pay Attention to this person's Interests, but you might select something like a Beautiful Flowering Plant for someone who keeps a few Violets on her desk, or a Nice Calendar, or an Elegant Desk Clock. We don't think you should get something Totally Impersonal or Too Utilitarian, like one of those plastic mats that goes underneath a Rolling Desk Chair (in fact, a Good Rule would be that if you can Order It from the Company Supply Catalog, it's not a Good Present). But we wouldn't choose something *Too* Personal, either. In a Typical Office, articles of clothing or jewelry aren't the best idea. And absolutely everywhere, Massage Oil would be a Big Mistake. Also, passing on the Fruit Gift Basket that you *just* received from *your* Boss to Your Assistant is Just Plain THOR, especially if you try to Pass It Off as Your Own Gift, rather than, "Oh, George just gave me this, and I hate oranges, but I know you like them; would you care for this? Oh, and while on the topic of presents, here's my little gift to you! Merry Christmas, Louise!" Note: Be certain that George does not bear witness to this transaction, or you trudging out to your car sans basket, or Louise trudging out to *her* car *avec* basket, or you'll be in Big Trouble. (See pages 167–168 for more on "Regifting.")

The Etiquette Grrls also think it would be a Smart Idea to purchase a few Small Items and Wrap Them so they're at the ready if someone comes by with an Unexpected Gift for You and you wish to Reciprocate. Good Chocolates, Scented Candles, a Bottle of Particularly Good Wine—it's nice to have these on hand. If you don't need them, then consider them little presents to yourself, to be opened Après the Holidays.

WEDDINGS

Yes, if you receive a Wedding Invitation, you should Send a Gift to the Happy Couple—even if you will not be able to Attend Their Nuptials. However, the EGs have Had It Up to Here with people who believe it's okay to send a gift up to a year after the Wedding! That, Dear Reader, is Nothing But Procrastination, and we Frown Upon It. Even if you're Terribly Busy, we think there is No Reason you can't find time to Duck Into a Shop and select an Appropriate Gift, and have the shop Ship It so that it arrives before the Wedding. We suppose that if the reason you're missing the Wedding is because you are Overseas, or something, and you plan on seeing the couple when you return two weeks after their Wedding, it would be okay for you to wait to give them their Gift in person, but really, if you're actually planning to Attend the Ceremony and Reception, we think you could squeeze a Quick Shopping Trip into Your Schedule.

Of course, the idea that you should spend approximately the same amount on your gift as you think the Reception Costs Per Person is Utter Hogwash. First, Dear Reader, the EGs think such Quid-Pro-Quo Gift Giving is Extremely Unseemly. You are Giving a Gift to a Couple to celebrate the Joyous Occasion of Their Wedding, not Paying Admission to the Reception! Give according to Your Means, always. The EGs think that any Well-Mannered Young Couple would be much happier to know that you put a bit of effort into selecting Vintage Guest Towels at a Flea Market than to have you go into debt for Candlesticks from Tiffany, even if the Young Couple had their Reception at The Plaza! (If a Young Couple does not Feel This Way, then you should send Their Address to the EGs, and we will make them sit in the hallway and write out the dictionary definition of "Greed" five hundred times. Maybe the Multiplication Tables, too, and a few Complete Conjugations of Latin Irregular Verbs for good measure.)

Not that the EGs wish to sound like A Broken Record, but whatever gift you select for the Happy Couple, it should Suit Their Taste. Must you buy something from Their Registry? Of course not. Many couples do not register at all, and even if a couple does, you are absolutely not obligated to choose from it! However, while it's lovely to give an Unusual, Creative Gift, just because Your Home in California is decorated in a Hawaiian Theme does not mean the couple has the same vision for their New England Colonial home, so it would be rather inconsiderate of you to assume they could use a Large Set of Tiki Mugs with Matching Torches. If for some reason you are Unsure of Their Taste (perhaps you are a Cousin of the Groom, but have not seen him since you were both ten years old), you'd be wise to err on the side of The Conservative and The Simple. A very plain glass vase can blend with almost any décor—and you can find nice ones in many stores, from Crate & Barrel to Shreve, Crump & Low. It's also smart to think in terms of Sets of Things, if you can. One demitasse cup isn't likely to do the couple Much Good, but a set of six would be lovely, even if they don't match any other china the couple owns. No fair giving something that obviously only one member of the couple will be able to appreciate, either—for example, a Pair of Earrings would be terrific for the Bride, but what is the Poor Groom supposed to do with them? Do not, however, assume that you must give the couple Something For Their Home. While those gifts are nice, and often Quite Useful, if you know the couple would appreciate a Series of Theatre Tickets, or Season Tickets for their Local Sports Team, feel free to go with that.

GIFTS FOR OTHER WEDDING-RELATED EVENTS

- If you are invited to an Engagement Party, you need not bring or send a Gift. Don't let anyone tell you otherwise, either.

- If you are invited to a Bridal Shower, and it has A Theme, it's nice, but not obligatory, to Go Along With It. For a Linen Shower, sheets, towels, tablecloths, etc., are all lovely. For a Kitchen Shower, a nice Fiestaware Teapot, a set of Nice Juice Glasses and a Pitcher, some of those Nesting Mixing Bowls, a copy of Your Favorite Cookbook, and so on, make great gifts. The EGs do *NOT* approve of Lingerie Showers, however. *Ugh!* If you cannot attend a Bridal Shower, you should send your gift to the home of the person hosting the shower, so that the Bride-to-Be may open it during the Festivities. Certain people, such as The Bridesmaids, may be invited to more than one shower if there are a few thrown in Different Cities, but no one needs to give more than one Shower Gift.

- What if the Bride and Groom have a Very Small Wedding, with only their Immediate Families in attendance, and you are not invited? You may certainly send a Gift, if you choose, but it's Entirely Optional. The EGs would say that if you typically exchange Holiday or Birthday Presents with someone, it would be nice to send a Wedding Present to them even if you're not invited to their Wedding because it's Extremely Small, or Far Away.

BABY GIFTS

The EGs absolutely *adore* shopping for Presents for The Wee Ones! There is absolutely nothing so adorable! When Our Dear Friends and Family Members are Expecting, we become Obsessed with shopping for the Perfect Baby Gift!

- Baby-Shower Gifts. Okay, everyone, let's Get This Straight. One throws a shower for one's Sister's, or Dear Friend's, *FIRST CHILD. One Shower per Mom.* Why? Because, Dear Reader, the purpose of the Shower is not to Get a Truckload of Presents for the Baby. Au Contraire! The purpose of the Shower is to provide a First-Time Mother with Advice and Items She Absolutely *Needs* for her child! Obviously, a First-Time Mother is not going to have a High Chair Lying Around just in case she Becomes Pregnant, so it makes sense for her Close Friends and Family to help her with such a purchase. However, the EGs think it is in no way a Slam on Second-, Third-, Fourth-, even Fourteenth-Time Moms to not give them a Shower, as they will have clearly had the Good Sense to store the Baby Items from Their First Child. And the EGs aren't putting up with that "But what if the crib I had for Little Tommy isn't considered safe anymore for Little Suzy?" argument. *Obviously,* if something is Unsafe, you should Go Buy Another One—there is Nothing Stopping You from stepping into a Furniture Store and Buying a Crib Yourself. It's not Your Friends' fault that the one they gave you five years ago doesn't meet the Current Safety Standards, and they do *NOT* owe you a Replacement! If you were so shortsighted as to Throw Away items from Your First Baby's Shower, then, also, you should simply Replace Them Yourself. And furthermore, it doesn't matter One Bit if Your First Child is a Boy and Your Second Child is a Girl. Believe the EGs, a Nice, Soft Baby Blanket is a Nice, Soft Baby Blanket, and no baby is going to Give a Damn whether it's Blue or Pink! Babies can't even discern colors for A Good Long While! Better yet, pick a gender-neutral color for Baby's Nursery/Layette/etc., like green or yellow or beige or grey (hee, hee!). Obviously, ivory and white are always good, too. This is true even if the Mother thinks she knows the Baby's Sex—those tests have been known to be Wrong! Also, do not Monogram Anything for the Baby before it is Born. Parents have been known to Change Their Mind and NOT name their Wee One Algernon, as they has previously sworn they would definitely do. Furthermore, there is Nothing Wrong with hand-me-downs, and this is another reason not to run around Monogramming everything for Le Petit Chou. New Baby does not need An Entirely New Wardrobe, and guess what, Dear Reader? The Wee One will not know or care if The Baby Blanket is Brand-New or Twenty Years Old! In fact, in the EGs' homes, hand-me-downs were *cherished* (which is probably where the EGs developed their fondness for Vintage Clothing and Old Books and Toys). Also, we're not at all keen on holding a Baby Shower before the Baby is born, as sadly, we know that too many things can Go Tragically Wrong, and then someone is stuck with all the Shower Gifts as a Reminder, which is Just Horrible.

- Whew, the EGs are Un Peu Worked Up! However, let us now Move On to what you should give a First-Time Mother at her Baby Shower. Because of what we have said above—that a shower is to provide the Mother with items she clearly needs for her Baby, and that they should be expected to serve for any future children she might have—the EGs think you should always purchase serviceable, durable, well-made Shower Gifts.

- Gifts for a Newborn Baby. You might find a Darling Outfit for the Wee One, or the Softest Blanket Ever, or an Adorable Bib. You might purchase a Silver Rattle, or a Silver Frame, engraved with the Baby's Name and Birthdate. Or a basket of Baby Soaps and Lotions and Adorable Wee Washcloths! There are so many possibilities! If the Newborn has An Older Sibling who's still Young Enough to Consider Him- or Herself the "Baby," it might be thoughtful to send a Book or a Small Toy to that child as well. Even if you do not send a Gift, do send a Note conveying Your Best Wishes to the Newborn and his or her Parents.

- Send Flowers to the Mother. Well, this is customary, but the EGs think it might be nice to send a Real Present that the Mother can enjoy. After all, gone are the days of a New Mom recovering in the Hospital for a Week, since these days hospitals Throw You Out On Your Ear one day after you've had Major Brain Surgery, much less had a Baby! You wouldn't want to send Flowers to the Hospital and have the Poor New Mom have to lug them home in addition to the Baby, now, would you? The EGs think a Really Good Book, or a Gift Certificate for a Pedicure, or even the promise of a Lunch Date as soon as she's Up and About make lovely presents, too.

- Presents from Godparents/guests at the Christening. Obviously, it is Quite an Honor if you're asked to be a Godparent or to attend a Solemn Occasion like a Christening (or a Bris). You should take a Gift that is In Keeping with the Solemnity of the Occasion—please, no Stuffed Animals or Gap Baby Booties. Choose a vintage bank, a child-size Place Setting of the parents' Silver Pattern, or something else that will Stand the Test of Time.

HOUSEWARMING GIFTS

Honestly, one of the best Housewarming Gifts is an offer to assist the New Homeowner (or New Apartment Renter) with Moving and/or Renovating. If this isn't possible, you might choose a Nice Potted Plant, or some books on Decorating, or something the New Homeowner could use that was not necessary in their Prior Dwelling. For example, for a friend who's just Purchased a Home after years of Yardless Apartment Living, a set of Gardening Tools would be ideal.

WHEN YOU ARE A GUEST AT A DINNER PARTY
It's lovely to Bring or Send Flowers, or to have them sent the day afterward. You may bring a Box of Chocolates, or a Bottle of Wine, but do remember that the Hostess is under no obligation to serve them that evening.

ANNIVERSARY GIFTS
It's very nice to remember the Anniversary of Very Close Friends, or Family Members, but the EGs think you needn't give Anniversary Presents to every Married Couple You Know, every single year, unless you have oodles of Time and Money at your disposal. But really, this is Up to You, depending upon how close a relationship you have avec the couple. If one is going to send an Anniversary Gift, the Etiquette Grrls think it'd be Really Smashing to look to the traditional list of Anniversary Gifts for Inspiration. Here it is, for Your Edification:

First Anniversary	Paper
Second Anniversary	Calico, or in some regions, Any Cotton will do
Third Anniversary	Leather or muslin
Fourth Anniversary	Books or silk
Fifth Anniversary	Wood or clocks
Sixth Anniversary	Iron
Seventh Anniversary	Copper, bronze, brass, or wool
Eighth Anniversary	Pottery or electrical appliances
Ninth Anniversary	Pottery Again (Why? The EGs have No Idea, except that one can never have Too Much Pottery, and perhaps one received An Electrical Appliance the year prior.).
Tenth Anniversary	Tin or aluminum

Eleventh Anniversary	Steel
Twelfth Anniversary	Silk (again) or linen
Thirteenth Anniversary	Lace
Fourteenth Anniversary	Ivory
Fifteenth Anniversary	Crystal
Twentieth Anniversary	China
Twenty-fifth Anniversary	Silver
Thirtieth Anniversary	Pearls
Thirty-fifth Anniversary	Coral or jade
Fortieth Anniversary	Ruby
Forty-fifth Anniversary	Sapphire
Fiftieth Anniversary	Gold
Fifty-fifth Anniversary	Emerald
Sixtieth Anniversary	Diamond
Seventy-fifth Anniversary	Diamond

If you are invited to a twenty-fifth, fiftieth, or seventy-fifth anniversary party, you should bring or send a gift, although, of course, you are under no serious obligation to march out and purchase Something Pricey. Your presence (no pun intended) at the party should be a gift in and of itself for the couple. However, if you do bring a gift to Mr. and Mrs. Elderly Neighbor's Fiftieth Anniversary Party, you need not go out and buy a gilt tea service. (In fact, we beg you not to!) Decorative items for the couple's home, or tickets to an Upcoming Performance they'd enjoy, make ideal presents for these Milestone Anniversaries.

GIFTS FOR CHILDREN
The EGs have Had It Up to Here with unnecessarily expensive Presents For Children! Now we are all in favor of gifts that will,

one day, be Cherished Keepsakes (e.g., Silver Baby Cups and the like), but we do not think there is *any* reason to give a Small Child anything from Gucci, one of those Über-Expensive Miniature Cars, a $2,000 Robot Pet, etc. Toddlers shouldn't be Encouraged to be Pretentious! There is a reason that traditional toys such as Dolls, Blocks, Lincoln Logs, Lego, Dollhouses, Model Airplane Kits, Stuffed Animals, etc., have been popular for ages—it's because Kids Love Them! And one should Never Hesitate to purchase books for children. If they're too young to read, their parents can read the books to them.

JUST A REMINDER—YOU GET A GIFT, YOU WRITE A DAMN THANK-YOU NOTE

And the Etiquette Grrls do mean that you must Take Pen to Paper. We don't mind if you use e-mail to send a quick thank-you message to the friend who gave you a Quick Lift to the Train Station yesterday, but if you receive a Gift from someone, you absolutely must write a real, old-fashioned Thank-You Note. Please refer to chapter 3 on Letter-Writing to see examples of Thank-You Notes for several different types of presents.

HOSTESS GIFTS

It is a Long-standing Rule of Etiquette that if you are an Overnight Guest in someone's home, you must arrive with a Small Gift for Your Hostess. (Technically, you also have the options of sending something along after you depart or of Having Flowers Delivered, but the Etiquette Grrls think it's swell to arrive with a Wee Present in Hand.) What, however, makes for a Good Hostess Gift? For starters, Dear Reader, put a little thought into this gift. Sure, you could probably pick up a carton of Marlboros and a six-pack of Bud Lite with a minimum of effort, but the Etiquette Grrls highly doubt Your Significant Other's Mother will appreciate such bounty. If you know Your Hostess has a Sweet Tooth, a box of Good Chocolates would be lovely. Is she Mad About Her Garden? Then a Pretty

Flowering Plant would make an ideal present. If you don't know much about her at all, there are a number of Safe Gifts that are good for almost anyone:

- A pretty scented candle. Or a box of very good quality unscented tapers (everyone who entertains can always use them). You might include a Candle Snuffer for an extra touch, or some matches in a Vintage Box.

- A basket of bath salts, soaps, gels, etc. The Etiquette Grrls personally love products by Fresh. Oh, would that Everything in the World smelled like their Lemon Sugar or Honey Linden products!

- A specialty food item that your hometown or region is Known For. A New Englander visiting a friend in Charleston might bring a small tin of Yummy Maple Syrup, or a box of Maple Sugar Candy. A guest from London could present His Hostess with an assortment of Delicious Teas from Fortnum & Mason. A pretty coffee-table book about The Region/Town/Country from whence you came is nice, too.

- A really keen, inexpensive option: Homemade Pastry. We can't think of *any* hostess who wouldn't adore a freshly baked loaf of Your Special Raisin Bread, or a nice batch of Chocolate Chip Cookies.

Another thing: It's very thoughtful (though not, of course, obligatory) to bring a Little Something for the Hostess' Children. We think Books are perfect for this—heck, Those Young Kids Need to Read More! Literacy is Super-Fly! There are so many Lovely Editions of Children's Books nowadays that finding appropriate ones should be easy, not to mention a pleasure. (The EGs personally love to give *Make Way for Ducklings* to any child who doesn't already have it.)

"REGIFTING"

Ever since that *Seinfeld* episode, people are paranoid about Regifting. Can you do it at all? Technically, we suppose it is possible to Regift, but it's such a Rotten Hassle that we don't ever do it. Do any of the following situations apply to you, Dear Reader? If so, then we're sorry—put the Ugly Vase in the closet and Move On With Your Life.

- If you can't remember who gave it to you, you're not allowed to give it to anyone else. It would be the Faux Pas of All Faux Pas to give someone a gift they'd actually given you!

- If you've Used It, you should Keep It. No one wants a candlestick caked with old wax, or the dog-eared paperback copy of *A Portrait of the Artist as a Young Man*, complete with Your Marginal Notations, that you used five years ago in your Twentieth-Century-Lit Course.

- If it's Monogrammed with Your Initials, or Otherwise Personalized for You, you're not allowed to give it to anyone else. (Except, of course, as a Bequest. After you've Passed On, your grandchildren will love the Cigarette Case engraved with your initials and the initials of the Beau who gave it to you. Your Roommate, however, would be Rather Perplexed to receive it. Unless, of course, Your Roommate went on to marry the cigarette-case-giving Beau, à la Eloise in J. D. Salinger's story "Uncle Wiggly in Connecticut," in which case such a gesture would certainly be a Final Jab from Beyond the Grave.)

- If it's a unique, or at least unusual object, and there is the Slightest Chance the Original Giver will see it in the New Owner's Home or, if it's clothing, On Their Person, you must keep it.

- If someone created it Especially For You, you have a Moral Obligation not to regift it. Perhaps the Original Watercolor

Painting by Your Aunt Annette doesn't quite pick up the accent color in Your Throw Pillows, and this bugs you, but you shouldn't turn around and give the painting to someone else. It's not a good idea to attempt to sell such an item, either, should Auntie walk into Your Gift Shop one day and see it, or find it herself up for grabs on eBay.

- Never, Ever, *EVER* pass off an article of your clothing to a Friend or Acquaintance with a reason like, "Since I lost all that weight, this doesn't fit me, but I think it's big enough for *YOU*."

- If, despite Our Best Advice, you decide to pass along that Cake Plate you received as a Wedding Present, then, for the Love of All Things Holy, make certain you've removed any evidence that you received it as a gift! One EG's Mother received a Wedding Present from her cousin "Lily" that had, nestled in the tissue paper inside the box, a Gift Card that read "From Alexandra to Lily—Happy Birthday!" Dear Reader, you've Been Warned.

When is Regifting okay? Well, the EGs don't approve of Regular, Run-of-the-Mill Regifting, but we do recognize some Special Circumstances. Let's say Your Late Grandmother gave you several Linen Tablecloths from Her Collection before she died. Now, your niece is getting married, and you'd like to give one of the Tablecloths to her. That's perfectly fine, Dear Reader! That's not Regifting—it's Passing Along an Heirloom!

NO, YOU MAY NOT "REGISTER" AT SEPHORA FOR YOUR TWENTY-FIRST BIRTHDAY

All right, Tout Le Monde, listen up. The Etiquette Grrls believe this whole business of Registering for Gifts has gotten rather insanely Out of Hand. Everywhere we go, from Target to Tiffany's, we are offered the opportunity to open a Gift Registry! Now, mind you, the Etiquette Grrls aren't All That Keen on Wedding-Gift Registries, but those, at least, have been around a while, and some people do say they appreciate knowing the Bride's China Pattern, or what have you. (The EGs are reserving their venom re: Greedy Brides for a Future Volume in which we can cover this subject in detail, Dear Reader, so forgive us for skipping it here.) However, we would like to state emphatically that it is not, Under Any Circumstances, acceptable to register for Your Birthday, or Your Six-Month Anniversary, or Your Housewarming Party, or Your Kid's First Communion, or Because It's Thursday, or Because You Have a New Kitten. This, Dear Reader, is Just Plain Greedy. Surely anyone who is close enough to you to have the desire to Buy You A Present for any of these occasions knows you well enough to Pick Something Out By Himself.

Small Children, especially, have No Business registering for anything, no matter what those Giant Chain Toy Stores would have you believe. Yes, we agree that your wee one's Christening, Bar Mitzvah, or First Birthday is a very special occasion, but you need not Take It Upon Yourself to specify exactly which PlayStation 2 games Junior wants, or that Susie only wants toys emblazoned with the *Redheaded* Powerpuff Girl, because she's Deathly Afraid of the other two. For God's Sake, it's an Important Learning Experience for Junior and Susie to receive a gift they consider Boring, like, say, a Fair Isle Sweater, have to smile and graciously thank the Giver, and write a Proper Thank-You Note. Do you really want to raise a Nasty Little Veruca Salt Type? We sincerely hope not.

NO, YOU MAY NOT ASK FOR MONEY IN LIEU OF GIFTS

Gee, greedy much? Yes, perhaps your Rent Is Due, and you could really use Cold, Hard Cash instead of Assorted Presents for your upcoming birthday, but to suggest this to anyone is Terribly Rude. When something nice happens to you, your Dear Friends and Relatives want to give you a present you'll remember. Whether it's something they make themselves or take special care picking out,

chances are they really enjoy taking the time to get the Perfect
Present for you. The Etiquette Grrls always do! We'd be Quite
Insulted if someone asked us to just Fork Over a Fifty instead of
scouring Antique Shops for the perfect Vintage Compact for her!
This also extends to the Nauseous Practice of "Money Trees" at,
say, College Graduation Parties. Ugh! The EGs think that if you'd
like to give someone a gift, go ahead and give them a gift—feel
free to ignore the Request for Cash, or the silly "Money Tree."
You're not being Rude; the Greedy People are, and the EGs give
you permission to Rise Above Them. Might we suggest that a Copy
of This Book would make a great present for such people? Perhaps
with a Nice Bookmark placed at this very page?

NO, YOU MAY NOT ASK GUESTS TO PAY FOR THEIR OWN MEALS IF YOU'RE THROWING A PARTY AT A RESTAURANT

Dear God! The mere fact that people would even *consider* doing
this is enough to make the EGs Reach for the Gin! If you have
someone as a guest in Your Home, you wouldn't expect them to
pay up for the Food and Beverages they consumed, would you?
(Needless to say, the EGs *SINCERELY* hope your answer to that is,
"Of Course Not!") Now, if the venue changes to a restaurant, you
are still The Host, and you are required to Pick Up the Tab for all
of your guests. We are sick and tired of hearing about people who
want to throw a Big, Swanky Party at a Nice Restaurant for someone, but don't want to Pay For It. If you can't Foot the Bill at
Chez Posh for the fifty people you want to invite, here are your
choices:

- Invite fewer people.

- Change the venue to a restaurant that suits your budget.

- Host the party at your home—remember, a Modest Tea or a
  Backyard Cookout can be lots of fun, and much less expensive
  than a Restaurant Dinner.

No saying that everyone can "order whatever they want as long as each person's check comes to less than ten dollars," either.

For that matter, the EGs feel the same way about whether or not you should have an Open Bar at an event you host, *especially* at Your Own Home. If Alcoholic Beverages are available, the guests really shouldn't have to pay for them. If it's too costly to keep an Open Bar running at the party you've planned, there are plenty of things you can do to avoid making your guests reach for their wallets to pay for their drinks. You might have waiters pass trays of Pre-Mixed Cocktails instead of taking Individual Drink Requests (it's usually cheaper to mix big batches). You might choose to serve several varieties of Beer and Wine instead of Hard Liquor. You might have lots of interesting soft drinks—lemonade, iced tea, punches, etc.—and avoid alcohol altogether. After all, the EGs do love our G&Ts (with Bombay Sapphire, please), but if we accept an invitation to Your Bridal Shower, we're going because we want to see you, not because we want to Get Shellacked. That is what Bars are for, and we can all go to one afterward.

Questions and Answers on Various and Sundry

Dear Mesdemoiselles de Etiquette,

Hello again, mes dear filles! Comment sommes-nous? I have a few more tiny quandaries pour vous s'il vous plaît:

How should we feel about scotch? And Irish whiskey?

Well, I thank you for your time once again. Merci, les Mesdemoiselles de Etiquette!

Yours, sincerely,
Le Duc de Denver

Your Grace,

Why, how nice to hear from you again, Dear Duke. You are the Etiquette Grrls' Most Faithful Correspondent, indeed. As you are no doubt well aware, Dear Duke, the Etiquette Grrls' Favorite Alcoholic Beverage is Gin. We also are exceedingly fond of Pimm's, a positively smashing English Beverage. As for other drinks, we encourage any Traditional Drinks—Scotch and Sodas, Manhattans, Screwdrivers, Gimlets, and so on. In short, any drink that was likely to have been A Favorite of Your Dear Parents, Grandparents, and Generations Past is fine. Although the Etiquette Grrls suppose that if one traced The Drinking History of one's Famille Distingué back far enough, one could wind up embracing things like Mead and Hot Possets; which the Etiquette Grrls can't really say that they recommend. It's damned difficult to order a Hot Posset in A Bar these days, besides.

As ever,
The Etiquette Grrls

Dear Etiquette Grrls,

I am planning a dinner party and am having a difficult time with the guest list. As you probably know, it is not easy to prepare a fine meal for twenty people. There are people on my list whom I definitely want to invite, but there are about five whom I couldn't care less if they came. On top of that, there are a couple of people in particular whom I couldn't care less if they even existed! Not to be Blunt, or anything.

So . . . a problem has come up. Can I get away with not inviting The Whole Gang? Or could I possibly invite some people for dessert and post-feast cocktails but not dinner?

I don't want to hurt anyone's feelings, but I also do not want to Slave Over a dinner for people who will Get on My Nerves.

Please help,
The Hesitant Host

Dear Hesitant Host,

A Dinner for Twenty? Without Help in the Kitchen? Or Help Serving? The Etiquette Grrls politely wonder, Dear Reader, if you might, perchance, have ingested some Crack? Oh, we're just kidding, Dear Reader. But you must surely have a Larger Dining Room in Your Humble Flat than the Etiquette Grrls do! Twenty, huh? Wow. C'est un petit banquet!! We're quite amazed that you'd undertake something on this scale! A Dinner Party like this would be Trying for even the Etiquette Grrls, and, as everyone knows, we are Seasoned Hostesses! Would you consider holding two smaller fêtes, or, perhaps having a Cocktail Party? That way, you wouldn't have to worry about quite so many Logistical Details.

As for the People You Have to Invite But Don't Really Like, well, we've all been there. Usually, this happens when you must reciprocate for someone else's hospitality, or when It Would Be Rude Not To Invite the Entire Office, and similar situations. It would be impolite, we think, to invite some people to a full meal and others merely for dessert. And this makes us come back to the idea of a Cocktail Party, where you have the Power (and indeed, the Obligation) to Circulate! You'll fulfill your obligation to invite everyone, with much less agony all around . . . you'll have to spend far less time with those guests who get on your nerves, because there's always an ashtray to empty or a tray to pass. You could even serve the Etiquette Grrls' Famous Artichoke Dip!

However, Dear Reader, if you do decide to have A Large Dinner Party, you can always seat The People You Don't Much Care For at the opposite end of the table from yourself. You'll still have to make Polite Conversation with them, of course, but at least there will be a Buffer Zone.

Cheers,
The Etiquette Grrls

Dearest Etiquette Grrls,

Just a few questions today, Dear Etiquette Grrls: How should one feel about turning twenty-five? Is vingt-cinq a Nombre Chic or merely the beginning of Something Dark and Terrible on par with the Evil Empire de Gates? Why is it that ma fair cité did not celebrate the day of Ma Vingt-cinquième Année in Proper Fashion—say, a full-on Parade with Free Cocktails and Artichoke Dip for all the Elite? Why is it that I must put up with these sorts of disappointments on my twenty-fifth birthday? Does it have to do with John Elway? Does this mean that I have been replaced, subverted, undermined? He got a parade for winning un stupide match de football américain; have my people really fallen so far into the depths of folie gauche?

Well, of course I jest un peu. But seriously, mes amours, what is this sick and twisted infatuation with professional sports, and with those villains who champion said sports? Please tell me what are we to do about those who trounce about with football, basketball, and hockey jerseys upon their personages—both professionally and spectatorially (if I may Make Up a Word)?

And what about the consumption, and the condonment of consuming, cheap domestique light (sometimes referred to as "lite") beer? Oh, my wonderful Grrls de Etiquette, please offer me some solace, some paix d'esprit, in these matters. For, I feel as if the world has turned on me.

Yours, most sincerely,
Le Duc de Denver

Our Dearest Duke,

Let us begin by sending Happy Birthday Wishes, albeit un peu belatedly. The Etiquette Grrls are Simply Disconsolate to hear you sounding so Down Around The Elbows, Dearest Duke! The Etiquette Grrls are shocked that the Good People of Denver did not recognize your birthday in an Acceptable Manner! The Etiquette Grrls think that the Dear Duke is certainly as, if not more, deserving of a Parade as John Elway. We can sympathize with you, Dear Duke—one of us recently spent her twenty-fifth birthday chez elle, with a Crummy Pepperoni Pizza, and a fascinating program on A&E about the Martha Moxley Murder Case in Greenwich, and the day went by Unnoticed by Absolutely Everyone. It was Quite

Depressing, and we have a Sneaking Suspicion that it's all Downhill from here.

The Etiquette Grrls are in Complete Agreement with you about the place in which Professional Sports are held in Our Society and Culture. Sure, the Etiquette Grrls are not Completely Adverse to occasionally attending, say, a Red Sox game, or keeping an eye out for the results of the America's Cup, but are there not More Important Things in Life than the Super Bowl/World Series/NBA Playoffs/etc.? And why do these things always preempt our Favorite Television Programs for weeks on end? As for people who regularly wear all manner of clothing emblazoned with the logos of their Favorite Sports Team—it makes the Etiquette Grrls cringe, Dear Duke! In fact, the Etiquette Grrls don't like clothing emblazoned with the logo of anything—do you really need to Announce to the World that Your T-Shirt came from the Gap/Abercrombie & Fitch/Calvin Klein/etc.?

The Etiquette Grrls, as you can probably well imagine, Dear Duke, are not Big Beer Drinkers. We find "lite" beer to be Particularly Vile. Quelle Waste of Money!!! If you must drink beer, at least get your money's worth, and drink something More Substantial and Flavorful!!! The Etiquette Grrls also frown upon the abundance of Wacky Microbrew Beers that have appeared in Recent Years. Does one really need Cranberry-Raspberry-Fruit Punch-Kumquat-Flavored Beer? The Etiquette Grrls think not. And, of course, it goes without saying that one should never, ever, ever drink beer Out of a Can. Or a plastic cup, as it is, sadly, served in Stadia.

Fondly,
The Etiquette Grrls

Dear Etiquette Grrls,

In two weeks, my Educational Career will end when I graduate from a Prestigious College in the Midwest. (I also attended an Esteemed Prep

School in a Very Small New England State.) Is it acceptable to contact successful Alumni of my Esteemed Prep School and Prestigious College and see whether or not they have any open employment opportunities? What is a poor history major to do?

Thank you ever so much,
Guessing in Granville

Dear Guessing,

Congratulations on Your Graduation, Dear Reader! The Etiquette Grrls completely understand your nervousness about Finding Gainful Employment. We have heard that the Job Market is very strong these days, but frankly, the Etiquette Grrls, who hold degrees in The Highly Marketable Fields of English, Writing, and Art History, haven't really found it to be so. Sigh.

We also understand your hesitancy to "Network." A great many people get Very Pushy about this sort of thing, and it's Quite Unpleasant. But the Etiquette Grrls feel Quite Sure that you are not One of These People, Dear Reader! (None of our Dear Readers is!) Hence, you certainly may write a Charming and Well-Written Letter on Good Paper to any Successful Alumni of your school who you feel might be able to offer you Advice, or better, yet, A Good Job. In fact, the Etiquette Grrls have found the Alumni of their own Prestigious Colleges and Esteemed Prep Schools (one of which is also in a Very Small New England State, oddly enough) to be Most Helpful and Kind! We've found that Alumni are usually happy to offer Us Young People a Helping Hand, and not just in the Realm of Employment! A Kind Alumna of one school even helped one Etiquette Grrl find a Suitable Apartment when she went away to Graduate School, and once, a Rather Famous Alumnus of one Etiquette Grrl's Prep School offered both of the Etiquette Grrls some Very Helpful and Witty Advice about How They Should Acquire An Agent. But the Etiquette Grrls digress, as they are wont to do. Alas. The point is, Dear Reader, the Alumni of Your Prep

School and College are, more likely than not, Good People. And if one must Network, it's certainly better to Network with Good People (who are likely to, if not assist you in your Job Search, at least give you a cup of tea, or better yet, a Gin and Tonic, and maybe a little Moral Encouragement, to boot) than with Complete Strangers.

Cheers,
The Etiquette Grrls

CHAPTER SEVEN

Miscellaneous Matters of Importance Redux

How to Eat an Artichoke

Dear Reader, Artichokes are so tasty, it's almost Maddening! However, eating them requires a bit of Savoir Faire. Approach an Artichoke with Caution. The Artichoke is a spiny, thorny, thistle-ish thing, yet it is eaten With the Fingers. You grab one of the leaves and gently pull it away from the base. If there is aioli or melted butter to dip in, you may, at this time, dunk the bottom of the leaf in it. Next, you put the bottom of the leaf into your mouth and scrape the meaty part against your teeth, pulling it off the main part of the leaf, which is inedible. Now take the leaf and put it on the edge of your plate. (Under no circumstances are you to use a Knife and Fork upon the leaves of an Artichoke! That is simply Not Done!) You continue to eat the leaves in this manner, moving inward, until you have eaten them all and you see the "choke" of the Artichoke—it is the fuzzy thing in the very center. Do not eat the choke! Rather, at this point, take your Fork and scrape away the fuzzy stuff, placing it on the side of your plate. You have now revealed the real reason to consume an Artichoke (besides, of course, the Sport of It): the Artichoke Heart! Using a Knife and Fork, slice off bite-sized pieces of this, and eat them, dunking each piece in the Dipping Sauce if you like.

N.B.: Artichoke Hearts are the Main Ingredient in Artichoke Dip, but, unless one is un peu masochiste, one would not want to have to eat the large amount of artichokes needed to get enough Artichoke Hearts to make a Batch of Artichoke Dip. One would probably not have room to eat the Delicious Artichoke Dip, and that, Dear Reader, would be Too Sad.

The Etiquette Grrls' Favorite Party Themes

If truth be told, Dear Reader, the Etiquette Grrls aren't at all keen on Theme Parties. They're always unoriginal, and invariably can be counted upon to be silly and Not Worth the Effort. But, if only the Host could be a wee bit more Inspired in Selecting a Theme for his or her Theme Party, well, perhaps the Etiquette Grrls could be persuaded to Drop By for a drink or two. We offer the following suggestions:

The WPA Party—Form a breadline at the hors d'oeuvres table. Paint a mural. Complain about being A Poor Writer/Artist/ Actor.

The Cotillion Party—Come as a Famous Debutante of the Past (e.g., Barbara Cushing, Brenda Frazier, et al.).

The Brahmin Party—Get a Hah-vahd banner. Drop your "r"s.

The 1920s Expatriate Party—Because They All Loved Their Gin. Wear your Pearls down your back à la Sara Murphy.

The Post-Christmas Transform All The Pastel Clothing You Received As Gifts Into Appropriately Black Attire Party—Mix a Giant Batch of Rit dye in the bathtub. Hang many clotheslines; provide rubber gloves; remember to put down Drop Cloths.

The Official Preppy Handbook *Party*—Drink heavily. Wear madras. Have trivia contests based on the book. Get drunk and crank call Lisa Birnbach.

The Megalomania Party—Dress like Bill Gates, Donald Trump, or Pinky and the Brain. Have a contest for the Best Plan for World Domination. Attempt to carry it out.

When May I Chew Gum?

If, by "Chewing Gum," you mean "When may I, in a manner resembling a cow chewing cud, chomp upon a giant, watermelon-flavored blob of bubble gum, snapping, cracking, and blowing bubbles that pop all over my face," then the Etiquette Grrls' answer is, "Never." Unless you can chew gum imperceptibly (meaning, specifically, that no one else can see, hear, or smell it), then you shouldn't be chewing it at all. To chew gum conspicuously is Simply Beastly.

On the other hand, if you have mastered the art of chewing gum politely (and believe the Etiquette Grrls, very few people have), you may legitimately ask where it is acceptable to do so. If you are alone—driving, reading, etc.—then feel free to enjoy your Chiclets. If you are In Public, however, be more careful. When you are with a small group, you should always offer others a stick of gum before having one yourself. (You do this by passing around the pack and letting each person remove a stick . . . you do not take a stick out of its wrapper and hand it to someone else. This is disgusting.) We suggest you refrain from chewing gum whilst on the 'Phone, on a Date, at Work, in Church, or at any sort of Formal Occasion.

Please do not chew gum constantly (unless you are a Former Smoker who has Recently Quit, in which case you earn a Bit of Our Indulgence). Finally, dispose of your gum properly. How infuriating it is to plant one's New Manolo upon someone else's ABC gum! Dear Reader, think of the Etiquette Grrls' Expensive Shoes, and do not ever drop your gum where we (or anyone else, for that matter) might inadvertently tread upon it! Similarly, do not stick your gum underneath anything for someone else to encounter. The undersides of tables, desks, etc., don't look like wastepaper baskets, do they, Dear Reader? Then do not use them as such! Take your gum, wrap it in a tissue or in the wrapper it came in, and throw it away in the trash. We suppose you might swallow it, but, frankly, the thought sickens us.

The Etiquette Grrls' Rules to Live By

1. Never purchase *anything* (in particular, Household Items of any sort—e.g., silverware, china, crystal, furniture, rugs, fabric, etc.) with any of the following words in its name: Grand, Renaissance, Baroque, Victorian, Glamour, Hollywood, Atomic, Floral, Euro-Style, Rustic, Post-Modern, or the name of Any Specific Sort of Flower.

2. Buy low, sell high.

3. If it ain't broke, don't fix it. And don't try to break it, either!

4. Trust your Gut Instinct. Most of the Time.

5. By the time you graduate from college, learn how to do the following things: Launder your clothes (with nothing shrinking, bleeding, etc.); remove Common Stains; iron everything in your closet; fold T-shirts and sweaters properly; thread a needle; fix a hem; replace a button; cook at least one meal appropriate to serve to guests; operate a vacuum, mop, and assorted scrub brushes; have a basic familiarity with major brands of cleansing products, know what does what, and how to use them without hurting anyone.

6. Know how to prepare one recipe that is good for potlucks, etc. (May we recommend Our Artichoke Dip?)

7. Murphy's Oil Soap cleans almost anything.

8. Know how to figure a tip at a restaurant (or anywhere), even if you Are Not Good at Math.

9. Learn how to drink Real Liquor. And while you're at it, to Hold Your Liquor.

10. Nothing is Anachronistic about Kindness, Common Sense, Respect, or Courtesy.

"I Am AWOL Because . . ."

Thinking of Dropping Off the Face of the Earth? Well, Dear Reader, the EGs do not approve! If you're going to ignore your e-mail, leave your telephone off the hook, and disconnect your apartment's doorbell, or if you plan to Leave the Country in the Dead Of Night, then you *must* notify Your Dear Friends. Therefore, we have prepared this Handy Form—simply check all statements that apply, photocopy, and send to Everyone You Know!

1. _____ I have Enlisted, and have Shipped Out in order to Serve Our Dear Country.

2. _____ I suffer from Fugue State, and I have No Idea Where I Am. BTW, who is _____ [fill in blank], and why am I getting His/Her (choose one) Mail????? And who the hell are YOU????????

3. _____ There was a Terrible, Horrible, Accident during one of my sixty-hour workdays, and I am currently pinned underneath several servers that Fell On Me. Think All Limbs and possibly my Spine are Broken. Please send for Help.

4. _____ I moved to Montana on The Spur of The Moment, like Everybody Else, Stupid. Where *ELSE* would I be? (And no cell service there, of course—it's strictly tin-cans-and-string technology. Try Smoke Signals or Carrier Pigeons. Pony Express also good.)

5. _____ I am in A Never-Lifting Alcohol-Induced Haze. _____ (fill in w/ current month) is The Lost Month. Didn't you Get the Memo? I thought you were here, too, in Similar Haze. You're not???

6. _____ You know what I was saying about Relocating to the United Arab Emirates? You're getting a Pet Camel for Christmas.

7. _____ I have decided to Go Nouveau-Faux-Hippie, and am Devoting the Rest of My Life to Following Phish.

8. _____ I am being Held Hostage by captors who are forcing me to Do Their Hacking For Them at Gunpoint. The Cat Flies at Midnight. The Frost Is On The Pumpkin. Stonehenge, Stonehenge. Alert The Proper Authorities, please. Thank you.

9. _____ I have entered A Cloistered Monastery/Convent (choose one).

10. _____ I have Scurvy/Malaria/Typhoid/Consumption/ The Plague (choose all that apply), and am dying/dead (choose one).

11. _____ Missing? I'm not missing. I'm living in your coat closet because I was tossed out of my apartment! By the way, we're running low on Limes. Also, could you pick up some smokes when you go out to get Your Meds refilled? Thanks.

12. _____ The Harry Potter/*Star Wars*/Comic Book Hero du Jour movie just came out, and I've been camped out for weeks.

13. _____ I have been summoned to the Secret Underground Bunker in Sea Girt, New Jersey.

14. _____ I'm Drunk. After all, if I can't have a Good Stiff G&T every hour on the hour, the Terrorists have Already Won.

15. _____ I've been Kidnapped!!!! SEND HELP TO CAN-ADA ASAP!!!!

16. _____ I could tell you, but then I'd have to Kill You.

17. _____ Two words, baby: Sing-Sing.

18. _____ I'm busy pouring over back issues of *Gourmet* magazine and *Martha Stewart Living*, planning My Elaborate Thanksgiving/Christmas/Holiday (choose all that apply) Menu. Say, do you know how to make Jellied Cranberry Sauce From Scratch? Oh, Dear God, MUST also go Hunt Turkeys TODAY. . . . Oh, hey, didn't you say there was a Turkey Running Loose on the Chatham College campus awhile back? Is he Still There perchance? [If not November/December: So what if it's _____ (insert month), I'm planning ahead!]

19. _____ Am busy Salting Cod. More later.

20. _____ Have gone to Recreate Pilgrims Landing on Plymouth Rock. Later, Priscilla, Baby, Later.

21. _____ Am busy watching All of the Episodes of *Brideshead Revisited* back-to-back w/Aloysius. Be quiet and don't bother me. You *KNOW* how Seriously I Take *Masterpiece Theatre*!!!!!

The Official List of The Etiquette Grrls' Likes and Dislikes

We Like	We Don't Like
• Cashmere	• Wool that itches
• Chocolate Ice-Cream	• Rocky-Road Ice-Cream
• Good Books	• Trashy Books
• Warm Cookies	• Digital "Cookies"
• Urban Decay (the cosmetic company)	• Actual Urban Decay/Urban Sprawl
• The Theatre	• The Theater
• Artichokes	• Brussels Sprouts
• Small Soirées	• Huge Keggers
• Boodles Gin	• Bud Lite
• The Word "AWOL"	• People Going AWOL
• French Toast made from Brioche from the Algonquin Hotel, New York City	• Burnt, squishy, or soggy toast from The Toaster.
• English Muffins, torn apart to reveal their "nooks and crannies"	• English Muffins, sliced, so that all the "nooks and crannies" are Squished, and don't hold butter, jam, etc.
• The Rat Pack	• Packs of Rats

Movement

We are not all Ballerinas (thank heavens). However, it is important to move with a modicum of grace. You should not, for example, stomp about heavily, unless you are, in fact, a trained Kabuki performer (and then, *only* on stage). Neither should you sprint everywhere, particularly if you are formally dressed and not late. The

Winter Cotillion is not likely to have gone anywhere if you arrive five minutes later than you would if you ran there at top speed, and you will not arrive red-faced, puffing, and slick with your rank sweat. If you are running late for an event, simply slip in quietly when you do get there. (Better yet, make certain to leave yourself enough time that you will not, short of a Cataclysmic Event, be late in the first place.)

Some articles of clothing, particularly Shoes, seem to transform otherwise perfectly Graceful Girls into leaden-footed, teetering, hobbled creatures. Yes, of course it would be nice to be six inches taller, but you won't see the Etiquette Grrls running around and breaking our ankles in Spice Girl platforms, which are vile and passé anyway. Shoes are frequently very pretty objects, but if you cannot walk well in them, Dear Reader, please do not buy them. You will look, and probably feel, miserable.

The Etiquette Grrls Are Ready for Their Close-Up: Posing for Photographs

So you have done something Fabulous, Dear Reader, and The Press is clamoring at your door. Or perhaps you are announcing Your Engagement or Your Wedding, or you are graduating from High School. All of these things require you to sit for a photographic portrait, which can be an awkward, tacky, and potentially self-esteem-wrecking experience. Fear not! The Etiquette Grrls can help you Look Your Best.

First, make sure the Photographer is Competent. Look around his Studio. Is there a hideous, soft-focus portrait of what appears to be An Aging Showgirl? Do you see those nasty "reflective" photos that remind all of us of Unfortunate, Late-'70s Elementary-School Class Pictures? At the first hint of Poor Taste, Dear Reader, *run*! And it goes Without Saying that you should never, *ever* have your portrait taken in one of those Mall Photography Studios.

Second, Plan Ahead. Try to get your hair done just before you will be photographed, and make sure that your clothing is clean, pressed, and lint-free. Try to wear classic clothing and accessories; the Etiquette Grrls shudder to think about all those misguided high school Girls posing for graduation pictures in embroidered capri pants and handkerchief tops. Solid colors are good, as are non-shiny fabrics. (A tip: If there is any chance Your Legs will be photographed, make *certain* you are not wearing those vile, shiny, glossy stockings! They will add innumerable pounds!) In the same vein, while the Etiquette Grrls think that Trendy Makeup, in Moderation, can be fun to wear occasionally, we do not think you should be wearing Body Glitter in your Engagement Portrait.

We recommend you choose black-and-white over color film, if you have that option. Black-and-white photographs have Timeless Style; in a silver frame, they will look smashing for ages! Furthermore, fifty years from now, Your Grandchildren will enjoy looking at *you*, not what color Urban Decay eyeshadow you happen to have been wearing.

Make sure the photographer knows how to focus his or her camera. Remember, nothing screams "Glamour Shots" like fuzziness! Also, refuse to assume Ridiculous Poses, no matter how nicely the photographer asks. Boys: Please avoid the "I Am Pretending to Be a *GQ* Model" Look, wherein you remove Your Coat and toss it "casually" over one shoulder. Girls: Please avoid the "I Am Looking Back Over My Shoulder at You" Look, which does Most Unflattering Things to Your Neck.

THINGS YOU SHOULD NEVER, EVER POSE AVEC

- Foam Numerals (seen in most Tacky Graduation Photos)

- Animals (yes, we're sure your Pet Bunnies are cute; no, they don't belong in your Engagement Portrait)

- Beanie Babies

- Sporting Equipment

- Fake Backgrounds (the Etiquette Grrls wouldn't Be Caught Dead in a real farmyard; why would we want to pose in front of a fake one?)

- Any sort of hat provided by the Photographer (no, that fez isn't "funky," it's dumb)

- Your Cell 'Phone, Laptop Computer, Palm Pilot, Sega Genesis, etc.

- Anyone sporting a Mullet

Goth Etiquette

The Etiquette Grrls, perhaps not un peu surprisingly, can count a Fair Number of Goths and other assorted "Alternative" Sorts among our Dear Friends, Acquaintances, and Readers. In fact, the Etiquette Grrls, who are generally found Wearing Black, frequently spotted Sporting Their Docs, and who are always a Fetching Shade of Pallid—with nary a dab of that Goth Foundation from Manic Panic, mind you, Dear Reader—have been known to Run With This Crowd ourselves every once in a while. In fact, every year in the mail, the Etiquette Grrls get an invitation to the "Miss Goth Pittsburgh Pageant." (Something which intrigues us, but tragically, we have not as yet had the opportunity to attend. Alas, Dear Goth Reader, there's always Next Year!) And it makes us Quite Angry when we hear people make Derogatory Remarks about "Those Weirdos who are always wearing black." We find People who say such things to be Insufferably Stupid, and the Etiquette Grrls will allow our Dear Readers to Put Anyone they hear making such a remark about Goth Kids or Anyone Else In His Place.

Allow the Etiquette Grrls to recount a Wee Anecdote to Demonstrate the Point, Dear Reader. One stunningly gorgeous crisp Autumn Day, the Etiquette Grrls, who, you will recall, Dear Reader, are From New England, and a Dear Friend of ours, a très chic Madcap Manhattanite, were window-shopping in a Posh Shopping District of Pittsburgh, Pennsylvania. All three, as it happened, were Wearing Head-to-Toe Black. A Young Man, of College Age or Older, and accompanied by His Parents, was heading on the sidewalk toward the Etiquette Grrls and Our Dear Friend. When he reached Our Group, he Pointed Rudely, and said to his Parents in the Loudest Of Tones, "See, *that's* Pittsburgh's Version of *Those* Kind of People." And he Laughed Cruelly. The Etiquette Grrls resisted the urge to Deck The Moron, but rather, said icily as we Walked On, "No, Kind Sir, We *Are* Those People." The Rude Stranger gaped. The Etiquette Grrls wonder: Is it such a Good Idea to say Nasty Things to people who tend to wear things like Steel-Toed Docs, which the Etiquette Grrls guess would hurt A Lot if they Just Happened to make contact with Your Shin? We don't think so.

The Etiquette Grrls do have a Wee Word of Advice to Young Goths, however. Don't Overdo It. Remember, as always, Less is More. Filing your teeth into Wee Fangs and wearing a Spiked Dog Collar as a necklace is less Fearsome than it is un peu Amusing. Further, Goth is about A State of Mind, not How Many Piercings You Have. Can the Etiquette Grrls be Sullen and Badass while dressed from Head to Toe in Laura Ashley or Banana Republic? Mais, naturallement! When in such a Mode, would we be categorized by Any Passing Stranger as "Alternative?" Certainly. And can we be Sullen and Badass and Simultaneously be Polite, Courteous, Gracious, and Charming? You better believe it, Dear Reader—the Etiquette Grrls are All Things. And you can be, too, Dear Reader. Remember, Attitude is Everything.

Your Personal Appearance: An Update

Oh, Dear Reader, how Foolish the EGs are. We could not have Possibly Imagined that trends would sink to New Fashion Lows!

- **"Peasant Style" blouses, skirts, etc.** Not only is this baggy, frumpy, and silly, it is Terribly Unflattering to Practically

Everyone. Plus, we think it's Rather Oxymoronic when it's Expensive. We sincerely hope that in 200 years, *Vogue* is not promoting couture "Mall-Rat Style."

- **Misguided Patriotic Clothing.** The EGs, naturally, think it's Splendid that so many people really want to show Pride in Our Dear Country. It's High Time for this! Hurrah! However, the EGs would like to remind you, Dear Reader, that one should never, ever use The Flag as part of an article of clothing or, worse, as a Hair Accessory, and furthermore, it is not really in the Best Taste to run around in a Red, White, and Blue Bikini in the guise of National Pride. And if you're considering, say, a Red, White, and Blue Wedding Dress, we humbly suggest that you would Accomplish Much More if you chose a Simple, Plain White Wedding Dress and donated the difference in price to a Charity. Fly a Flag on Your House, and if anything, purchase a small, tasteful Flag Pin to wear upon Your Lapel.

- **Fishnets,** unless you're Dressing Up for Halloween. Colored fishnets, especially, are très, très tacky.

- **1980s revival clothing.** If you want to wear something with Shoulder Pads, find a vintage dress from the 1940s. Otherwise, it would really be to our Benefit, as a Society, if we could just all agree that Florescent Fabrics, Off-the-Shoulder Tops, Acid-Washed Jeans, and Multiple Scrunched-Down Socks were Not a Good Thing, because, quite simply, They Weren't, and thus, we should all just attempt to Forget About It Altogether.

- **"Princess"/"Star"/"Slut"/"Boy Crazy" shirts,** especially Glittery Ones. Please, leave them on the shelves of dELiA*s, and hopefully, they will Go Away.

- **That Denim That Looks Terribly Dirty,** even after being laundered. What is the Point of This? There are plenty of people wearing jeans that are Actually Dirty, and the EGs would like to do something about that—we do not need Banana Republic selling jeans that appear to have been Soaked for Weeks in Used Motor Oil.

- **Faux Broken-In Clothing.** Again, there are quite enough folks sporting jeans that are actually faded, creased, and tattered with age—they should Upgrade Their Wardrobes. Everyone else is Not Helping Matters by purchasing Pre-Aged Clothing.

- **Visible Corsets.** These are intended to function as Underwear, and therefore may only be worn Underneath Other Clothes. Yes, we all know that *Moulin Rouge!* had Interesting Costumes, but basically, the place was a Strip Club.

- **Extremely low-riding pants.** The potential for Disastrously Embarrassing Self-Exposure is just Too High.

- **"Thong Clips."** Jesus, Mary, and Joseph! Whatever Fashion Genius came up with this idea Ought to Be Shot.

- **Jeans worn *under* skirts or dresses.** You may wear *either* pants *or* a skirt, not Both At One Time, Miss Indecisive.

- **Fake ponytails, bangs, braids, etc.,** particularly those in Rainbow Colors that one may purchase at CVS. If you wish to determine how you might look with bangs, fine—you may select some Fake Bangs on a Comb and try them on in the Privacy of Your Own Home. However, we've seen too many Brunette Girls wearing Totally Unconvincing Blond Ponytails lately, and this looks Extremely Silly.

- **Glitter in Everything.** For the Love of God, there is no need to wear Sparkly Body Lotion *and* Glittery Eyeshadow *and* Shimmery Lipstick *and* an Iridescent Blouse!

- **Giant punky, spiky, grommetted, or studded belts,** especially when worn to "add contrast" to an otherwise Sedate or

Girlish Outfit. This does not make you look like you have an Interesting, Complex Personality. It makes you look like you have a Bizarre Split Personality.

- **Boys with Obviously Highlighted Hair.** Is Your Hairstyle found on any member of any Boy Band? Then, Dear Reader, throw out your Sun-In, and get thee to the Barbershop, stat.

Sex and the City *Is* Not *Something to Emulate*

The EGs despise this show! We do not understand why anyone would look to this show's Quartet of Idiotic Floozies as inspiration for Her Wardrobe (nevermind Her Moral Choices—we sincerely hope, Dear Reader, that You Know Better). No, it is *not* permissible to wear White Pumps with a Formal, Black Outfit, in the Middle of Winter, just because Sarah Jessica Parker did it first! Nor is it cool to wear a Cowboy Hat unless you are actually engaged in Cowboy Tasks, like Roping Steers or what have you. And there is No Need, ever, to sport a Tacky, Curlicue-Script Gold Necklace spelling out Your First Name. If you feel the need to Personalize Your Accessories, Dear Reader, we recommend getting a Plain Silver Keychain from Tiffany's and getting it Monogrammed.

Adieu, Burberry!

Sadly, the EGs must revise our opinion of Burberry. We used to *love* Burberry Raincoats—we adored them for years for their Pretty Plaid Linings! Then one day the EGs woke up to find Everyone, Everywhere sporting Burberry Plaid on All Items of Clothing! Skater Kids are wearing Burberry Mufflers! There are, horror of horrors, Burberry Plaid Bikinis! For God's sake, there's *even* a Burberry *BARBIE*!!! And it's not usually even real Burberry Plaid now, but Cheap Knockoffs on which the Scale of the Plaid is Wrong and it doesn't match up correctly at the seams! So, to our Great Chagrin, the EGs have put our Burberry Raincoats in storage. Note to Aquascutum: If you are having the Slightest Thought of following in Burberry's Footsteps, the EGs would like to Have a Word With You.

Seasonal Clothing Issues

Here is a Helpful Chart.

Item of Clothing	Can I wear it before Memorial Day?	How about after Labor Day?	Exceptions
· White Shoes.	· No.	· No.	· Brides and Nurses and Tennis Players at Clubs With Strict Dress Codes.
· Linen.	· No.	· No.	· None.
· Sandals.	· No.	· No.	· Monks.
· Shorts.	· No.	· No.	· Only if you're engaging in Athletic Activities.
· Straw Accessories (shoes, handbags, hats, etc.)	· No.	· No.	· None.
· Lilly Prints.	· No.	· No.	· None. There might be a Wintery Lilly Print, in a heavier fabric, but if so, the EGs haven't Seen It.

There! Isn't that Helpful?

The EGs would just like to add that we have Heard the Voices of Our Dear Southern Readers, and others in Hot Climates. We understand that if it hits 95 degrees in October, a nice Linen Shift Dress might be the most tolerable item of clothing in Your Closet. To this, we say that we will allow you to Bend the Rules a Teeny Bit—as long as your outfit still does not scream "*SUMMER!*" A Linen Dress in Chocolate Brown, worn with Brown Slingbacks, will look much more appropriate than the same dress in a Yellow Floral Print worn with Sandals. The White Shoes, however, just Need to Be Put Away. Why? Because we said so. And honestly, Dear Reader, as we've pointed out above, White Shoes aren't really nec-essary with any outfit, except Bridal Gowns, Nurses' Uniforms, and Tennis Whites. If you're wearing a Light-Colored Outfit, Bone or Tan Shoes will usually look *much* better than White. The EGs really do not understand why this is Such An Issue for People!

Similarly, Velvet, Boots, Fur, and Leather are worn *ONLY* during Cold Weather. Even if it's Un Peu Chilly at that August Wedding on Cape Cod, you should not wear a Velvet Dress to it.

Update on Electronic Etiquette

Ah, Technology! Every day, it seems, there is a Brand-New Gadget, or a New Feature of One's E-Mail Program, or yet another thing one can do on One's Cell 'Phone. The Mind Boggles! Although we covered E-Mail and Cell 'Phone Etiquette in Our First Book, the Etiquette Grrls felt it necessary to revisit This Topic to account for Innovations in the Field. After all, it would be Terribly Rude of us to be Behind the Times.

INSTANT MESSENGER

This program is Genius! The EGs cannot praise Instant Messenger enough! First, of course, it is a Very Convenient means of com-municating in a busy office, when you just have a Quick Question that's not worth an e-mail or phone call ("What time's the Meet-ing?"). This, Dear Reader, is Your Justification for using Instant Messenger (frequently called "IM") constantly whilst At Work! And, what's better, you can talk with friends or coworkers about Totally

Non-Work-Related Topics, and look Perfectly Industrious—after all, you'll be Typing Away! You can plan where to meet Your Best Friend for dinner practically under the nose of Your Annoying Boss—she cannot Eavesdrop! Oh, Dear Reader, if you don't have IM, put down this book Right Now and Go Install It! Not that the Etiquette Grrls, of course, approve of your not devoting Your Full Time and Attention to Your Job. (Wink, wink.)

First, you will need a Screen Name. Make certain to choose one that is not Embarrassing or Juvenile, especially if you intend to use IM at work. In that case, you might want to use some variation on Your Name. However, if you have a Quirky Workplace, or if you'll only be using IM with Friends, be as clever as you please!

Second, you will need a Buddy Icon. There are tons of these available online, or you can make your own in PhotoShop, but again, consider whether this Accurately Reflects Your Image. Does a photo of a Bottle of Malt Liquor really seem appropriate for Your Office? Probably Not, Dear Reader.

Third, you will need to Format Your Text. We like the idea of choosing a font that's A Little Different from the Default Times New Roman, but not something that's Insanely Quirky Looking, like "OPTI DRACULA," which would Look Ridiculous if used for Several Paragraphs straight. Also, keep the color legible (there are Better Choices than light beige on white), and for heaven's sake, there is no need to have hot-pink text on a bright red background.

We have a few more tips on IM Etiquette. Always take care not to get your IM windows Mixed Up if you have a lot of them open. You would not want to send Your Boss something like, "Dear God, I am so hungover!" If you're within Earshot of Others, either turn the sounds off or Wear Headphones, as the little IM noises can be Quite Irritating. And finally, while we understand that IM is designed for Quick Communication, and does not offer a Spellcheck Function, do try to send IMs that have at least Some Semblance of Literacy. Using too many of Those Silly Abbreviations (LOL,

using "2" and "u" instead of "to" and "you," etc.) is Quite Imma-
ture. Also, punctuation is a Good Thing. Use it.

No one seems to have Asked Us, but the EGs think that the
Developers of IM really ought to Get Cracking on making some
additional Emoticons (those little Smiley things). At Minimum, we
require the following:

- A Smiley with raised eyebrows, as if to say, "Hmm. That
  sounds Rather Suspicious."

- An angry Smiley that's Even More Furious than the Current
  Wee Mad One. We often need to express Pure Rage, and the
  Little Mad Face doesn't suffice.

- A Smiley suffering from Ennui.

- An Exhausted Smiley, perhaps with Circles Under Its Eyes.

- A Gin-Mad Smiley.

- An Ill Smiley, perhaps suffering from a Bad Headache, brought
  on by Office Stress and Horrible Fluorescent Lighting.

WEBPAGES

We think that much like the decor of your house, Your Webpage
is An Extension of You, and you should make a Concerted Effort
to Make A Good Impression with your page. It should be well-
designed, operable, and free of Spelling and Grammar Mistakes.
You should avoid Elaborate Fonts and any background that is
"busy" or Terribly Common, such as any of the faux marble designs. And all of those pseudo-tie-dyed-looking patterns are Simply
Hideous, and Are Not To Be Tolerated. Once you have selected a
nice, Subtle Background for your page, you should select a font for
your text that is simple and that is of a size and color that can be
Easily Read. The Etiquette Grrls think it is Terribly Rude to make
people wait, so we feel you should see to it that your page does

not take An Inordinately Long Time to download. You can see to this by avoiding huge .gif or .jpeg files, and by using JavaScript and Flash with discretion, if you must use them At All. We Highly Doubt that Your Website, which contains only Your Resume and a Links Page, needs a thirty-second Flash Intro. You should never, *ever* program .wav or .midi files to open automatically when someone opens something on your page. Someone might log on to your page while they are at work, and an unexpected, loud rendition of "Twinkle, Twinkle, Little Star" will undoubtedly draw attention to the fact that they are not currently engaged in a Work-Related Activity. The Etiquette Grrls don't think it's very nice to Rat On People, Dear Reader! It is also Terribly Rude to provide people with Erroneous Information, so you should be sure that all the links on your page are correct and operable. Furthermore, we feel that counters on Your Page are Utterly Unnecessary. The Etiquette Grrls don't really care what number visitor we are to your page, and if we *did* want to know, we would ask you. It is unnecessary to point out that someone is the one millionth visitor to your page, as this will undoubtedly make said visitor feel as if they have been "out of the loop," or that they are simply a Lemming. Likewise, by pointing out someone is merely the fiftieth visitor to your page you might, albeit inadvertently, make him or her feel that he or she is very "uncool" to be looking at such an unpopular page. You should also make certain that Your Domain Name is Easy to Remember and not Unduly Long to Type. "www.suzys20-seventhbirthdaaaaay_parTAY.com" is Unneccessarily Complicated.

Certain things about Webpages have just Gotten Out of Control, though! There is absolutely no justifiable reason for you to embed code that makes Your User's Cursor turn into a Flower! And though we're sure you're Proud of Yourself for figuring out how to make text Scroll or Blink, this is Quite Vexing to anyone who is trying to read it. Furthermore, the EGs are sure that a Special Place in Hell has been reserved for whoever invented those Vile Pop-Up Ads that Will Not Die and Always Seem to Lead to a

Casino Site or a Porn Site or an Offer to Buy a Spy Webcam. Arrrrgh! If, Dear Reader, you should ever Run Into This Person, kindly give him a Hard Smack in the Head with Your Handbag and tell him it's Compliments of the EGs. The Person Responsible for Flash Pop-Up Ads should also be Read the Riot Act, and perhaps forced to listen to Destiny's Child until his eardrums burst.

Finally, Websites that Require Registration have their place, but you should never, ever be obligated to reveal Personal Information like Your Income, Marital Status, Ethnic Background, etc. Sites that do this are being Terribly Rude, and it'll be a Cold Day in Hell before the EGs sign up with them. We can understand why an Online Banking Site might need Your Birthdate to Verify Your Account, but it's just as Rude to ask someone how much they earn on an Online Form as Over Cocktails.

USING THE WEB

So, Dear Reader, you have a Computer with an Internet Connection! Keen! You're off to use the Web—but first, we must caution you, Be Polite While Doing So!

It is Very Bad Manners to send Annoying, Inquisitive, or Irrelevant E-mails to people who operate Websites just because there is an "e-mail us" link. This link should be interpreted to mean, "Please e-mail us if you have something Important to Ask Us, or to Let Us Know About, such as, 'Do you ship to Canada?' or, 'I found a broken link on your site.'" It does not mean, "Send us Lots of Spam E-mail, ask us questions about Some Other Site we have No Affiliation With, complain about how you can't see our site in Your Favorite Browser (Netscape 1.0 running on a Mac Classic), etc." Also, Websites are Separate Entities! It would be as bizarre for you to go to, say, Expedia.com, and complain that you can't log in with Your AOL UserID and Password as it would be for you to walk into Barney's and ask why they won't take Your Charge Plate from Saks.

Also, do remember that as with all Electronic Things, the Internet tends to Have Problems. Unrealistic Expectations about this technology are causing thousands of people to Curse Abominably within the Earshot of Small Children and Elderly Nuns! The Horror! Dear Reader, Your Browser will crash, we guarantee it. A site you really enjoy, or simply Need to Access, will be Unreachable because they are Upgrading the Servers. A train will derail in New Jersey and cut cables, making it Impossible for You to Get Online at all. (Don't laugh, Dear Reader. This last one actually happened to one EG—her office had no net access for four days straight. It was Nightmarish.) We suggest you Make Allowances for this, so you do not Unreasonably Defenestrate Your Laptop or get caught without a Printout of Your Flight Itinerary. If it's online, and you need to Print It, Print It Now, or you may never have the chance again.

THE FACSIMILE ("FAX") MACHINE
Dear Reader, should you need to send or receive a fax of A Personal Nature, then you should take special care to be at the machine when it is transmitted. If you wander off, and someone else, say, Your Boss, for instance, finds Your Résumé or the offer letter you're getting for Another Job waiting in the fax machine, then it is Your Own Fault, and you may not berate the person who happened to find it when they come to you Asking Questions.

CELL 'PHONES, PART DEUX
Oh, Dear Reader, the Etiquette Grrls thought Cell 'Phones were Troublesome back in 1998. We had hoped they would become Less Obtrusive, that people would come to Cut Back on Their Usage . . . but, tragically, this has not Come to Pass. If anything, they have become even more Infuriating!

QUIT IT, FOR GOD'S SAKE, WITH THE DUMBASS RINGER NOISES
"Für Elise" was Quite Bad. Beethoven's Fifth, in a tinny, piercingly high-pitched rendition, was Maddening. Yet now, one can Down-

load New Ringer Noises—worse yet, New Ringer Noises created by Annoying Pop Groups—and assign a unique one to every single person calling! The EGs cannot set foot on the Subway without hearing an Abysmal Cacophony of Sugar Ray, "Thank Heaven for Little Girls," and "God Bless the USA"! It is Downright Sick and Wrong! If everyone would just put their cell 'phones on Vibrate, and place them in a pocket where this could be easily detected, should someone call, then the World, Dear Reader, would be a Better, Quieter, Calmer Place.

We would now like to have a word with Nextel, makers of Those Two-Way Radio 'Phones. What the hell were you *thinking*, Nextel? Is it not Bad Enough with people answering and talking on cell 'phones everywhere that you need to introduce something that makes an Annoying Chirp whenever someone talks into it? Something that people need to Yell Into in order to be heard, and that broadcasts the Caller's Voice on a Wee Speaker for Everyone Nearby's Listening Enjoyment? You, Dear Nextel, can See Us In Hell.

The Etiquette Grrls would like to Make It Clear that we understand Cell 'Phones are Here to Stay. They have even proved Quite Helpful to us in Diverse Situations—when lost, we can Call for Directions from the Safety of the Etiquette Volvo (see Chapter 1 for more on how to use a Cell 'Phone Whilst Driving). When we are online, Very Important Calls can still reach us. We just would like to remind everyone that Silence is Not a Bad Thing. You do not need to be Chattering Away with someone, *anyone*, just because you have Unlimited Minutes or something. You could Read a Book whilst On the Bus. You could have a Pleasant, Polite, Face-to-Face Conversation with the person sitting next to you, instead of making That Poor Soul listen to you babble about whether you should wear Pumps or Slingbacks to the Big Party. If you are so attached to Your Cell 'Phone, Dear Reader, nothing is stopping you from using it in the Privacy of Your Own Home or Office, where you won't disturb anyone else.

VIDEO GAMES

Now honestly, Dear Reader, the Etiquette Grrls could hardly be considered Gamers. The very thought of this is Quite Amusing! It is almost as preposterous as the thought of the EGs sitting around in the Etiquette Flat playing Dungeons and Dragons. Tee hee! That might actually make an Intriguingly Ironic Party Theme. (Pass the Twenty-Sided Dice!) Yet when we hear a never-ending barrage of bleeps, gunshots, buzzes, cannon fire, sirens, and endless loops of "music" that sounds like a Xylophone Gone Horribly Wrong coming from the Apartment Next Door at All Hours of the Day and Night, we feel we must offer some Commentary on the subject.

First, the noises that Issue Forth from your average PlayStation 2 are Much More Annoying, and for some reason, seem to Carry Better through Walls and Floors, than typical Television Dialogue. So turn down the volume, or Wear Headphones. Also, we remind you that you are not, in fact, Actually Playing Soccer, or Football, or what have you, and there is No Need for you to Stomp Around, particularly if you live Upstairs From Anyone Else. Also, should you Get Shot or something, you are Not Really Wounded, and you needn't Curse at the Top of Your Lungs.

We also are Rather Suspicious of Video Games attempting to Establish Themselves as a Legitimate Art Form. Yes, the Etiquette Grrls can see that potentially, one far, *far* distant day in the future, they may be as interesting as, say, A Good Movie, but for now, Dear Gaming-Mad Reader, believe us, most people will not be impressed with your prowess at Blowing Up Helicopters and Tanks or whatever it is you accomplish in your hours of playing Grand Theft Auto, so it would not be Très Wise to bring this up at the next Management Meeting, or at a Swanky Cocktail Party. Also, a wee note for Boys—we are answering on behalf of All Girls Everywhere—no, we do not find it Entertaining to watch you reenact the 1986 World Series while we Sit on Your Couch, Twiddling Our Thumbs. Actually, this is Mind-Numbingly Boring. In the Nascent

Stages of a Relationship, we highly recommend you put Your GameCube in Your Closet.

All of this Being Said, however, the Etiquette Grrls would be totally in favor of "EGs—the Video Game," wherein you would pick out a Stylish Outfit and wander the streets, giving every Rude Person you encounter a Good, Swift Kick in the Shins, and steering Acid-Washed-Jeans-clad, Mullet-Sporting People toward Banana Republic. Perhaps the EGs could be Motion Captured, so everyone could see *EXACTLY* how an Artichoke Should Be Eaten! But—sigh—we're not going to be Holding Our Breath for the Nintendo People to call.

Rude Questions

By God, are People Nosy! The EGs have had it up to *HERE* with people who think it's okay to ask how much money someone makes, or how old they are, or how much they weigh, or if they Color Their Hair, or if they've had Cosmetic Surgery, or when they're going to Get Around to Having Children, or how they voted in the Last Election—Enough is Enough! We suggest the following replies:

- "Why do you ask?" or "Why would you want to know that?" These are terrific, all-purpose deflections. Most people will Stammer. Let them Stammer for a minute, then say, "In my opinion, that's personal."

- Make Something Up. "I'm fourteen," said whilst quaffing a Stiff G&T, is good.

- Snidely give an answer that Reveals Nothing. "Hmmm. Oh yes, I voted for One of the Candidates."

- "None of Your Beeswax."

- "My, aren't *you* Rather Inquisitive."

- "I could tell you, but then I'd Have to Kill You."

Forgetting Someone's Name

Of course, you must Try to Catch Everyone's Name, to Remember It, and, of course, to Pronounce It Correctly in Speech and Spell It Correctly in Writing. Take this from the EGs, whose names, Lesley and Honore, are Frequently Mangled. There's no "ie" in "Lesley." There's no Accent Mark in "Honore," and it's not pronounced As If There Were One. It's really not that difficult! But the EGs Digress.

Should you make a mistake in Speech or Writing, and the person corrects you (gently, we hope, the way the EGs correct people— "Oh, actually, my name's spelled with an 'ey,' but don't worry about it," etc.), you should immediately apologize. ("I'm sorry—of course I know how to spell your name! My mind is One Big Lacuna lately.") More importantly, Dear Reader, you should memorize the correct spelling or pronunciation, so you never make the Same Mistake Again!

If you are Making Introductions and Draw a Total Blank—or if someone you don't recognize accosts you In Public and you have No Idea Who He Is—just admit it. "I am *SO* sorry, I am terrible with names—I've forgotten yours." When they tell you, again, make a note of it, and then try to say Something Mildly Amusing, like, "I don't usually do anything Quite This Stupid until I've had another six drinks or so."

Guests Who Bring Along Guests of Their Own

Okay, Dear Reader, let's be Emphatically Clear on this point: You are not allowed to assume that an Invitation you receive automatically is extended to Your Significant Other, Your Children, or any Other Members of Your Family or Social Circle. Sometimes, for very good reasons, these people, Dear to You as They May Be, are specifically not invited to parties, weddings, etc., and you have two choices: attend without them, or Send Your Regrets. However do you tell, though, if a Guest or Your Children May Accompany You? There is, in fact, a Very Easy Way to Tell: Read the Envelope!

"Mr. Alistair Crowley and Guest" means that you (assuming, Dear Reader, that you are Alistair) may invite a Date of Your Choice. You would R.S.V.P. to Your Hostess and tell her that you plan on bringing, say, Your Girlfriend, Winifred Trippleton. If Miss Winifred Trippleton receives an invitation that says, "Miss Winifred Trippleton and Escort [or and Guest]," she would do likewise, R.S.V.P.-ing to say that she will attend avec her Dear Boyfriend, Alistair.

However, what if Alistair receives an invitation addressed only to "Mr. Alistair Crowley"? Or if Winifred receives one in merely her name? Well, then, Dear Reader, if they wish to attend this event, they must go alone. They may not call up the Hostess and whine, attempting to extract an invitation for Their Significant Other. They must especially not resort to Childish Behavior, such as telling the Hostess, "Well, FINE, if Alistair's not invited, I'm not coming, either." The Hostess will obviously conclude Winifred is a Dependent, Weak Person, who is more interested in Hanging Out With Her Boyfriend than attending, say, the Wedding of One of Her Close Relatives, and she'll probably be glad you won't be there, if that's where Your Priorities Lie.

Now, Dear Reader, do bear in mind that if Your Hostess knows you have a Significant Other, she would not exclude him without having a good, and fair, reason for doing so. Perhaps Space Is Tight, or Costs Are High, and she has been forced to' choose between letting everyone bring a date and fitting in all the guests she personally knows and would like to be there. If this is the case, Dear Reader, you must accept it. (A note to Hostesses: Should you need to do this, you must do it fairly. It is not nice to allow your friend Hortense to bring a Date, while your friend Matthew may not, just because you think Matthew's Girlfriend is Quite Irritating and you fancy Setting Him Up avec your cousin Charlotte. Married Couples and Engaged Couples should always be invited together to Social Events, as should Couples Who Live Together, but you may draw the line there. If you're hosting a Wedding, you should always allow Members of the Bridal Party to bring a date, if they choose.)

The same thing goes for Children. An Invitation sent to "Mr. and Mrs. Alistair Crowley," does *not* mean their three small children, Priscilla, Hester, and Fitzwilliam, may Tag Along. If the Hostess had intended to invite the Youngsters, the invitation would have been sent to "Mr. and Mrs. Alistair Crowley and Family." If you wish to attend the event, you must have someone else Watch the Kids—you should not bring them along, and nor should you attempt to Obtain Invitations for them. Some people simply like to throw Parties for Adults Only, and if you have a Problem With This, then you must Send Your Regrets.

Again, a note for Hostesses: If you choose not to invite Children to your event, then please, for the sake of Your Own Sanity, choose a Cut-Off Age and Stick to It. (And do try, if you can, not to make the cutoff seem Evil. "No one under eighteen" or "no one under sixteen" is good. "No one under five," when several of Your Guests have one child under five and one over, is Rather Thoughtless.) Furthermore, remember, if you're having a Party at Your House and you don't wish Your Guests to bring their kids, your own Wee Ones ought not to be Running Around Underfoot.

As a hostess, if someone R.S.V.P.s for people You Didn't Invite, just give them a Quick Call and explain why you haven't room for extra guests. What to do if someone actually shows up at Your Party with a Date, or Children, whom you Didn't Invite and whom they didn't even R.S.V.P. for so you could Stop Them? Well, Dear Reader, you probably should just Grin and Bear It at this point. There's no point in Creating a Big Fuss . . . just try to accommodate the extra person as best you can. You might suggest that the child watch a video in the Other Room, so as not to be in the middle of things at your dinner party. Or, if it's a large event and you suspect lots of Unthinking Guests will bring Kids, you might hire a baby-sitter; you could then say, "Oh, I see you brought Little

Georgie along. We're not having kids at the reception, but the baby-sitter is down the hall to the right . . . after you've dropped him off there, come back and I'll introduce you around!" In the future, we'd make things Emphatically Clear to the Transgressors, if you ever invite them to Anything Else Again—put a Wee Note in their invitation saying, "Sorry we can't invite Little Georgie— not enough space—but we hope you two will come!"

PEOPLE WHO DON'T R.S.V.P.
You've invited eleven of Your Closest Friends to your house for a Saturday-night Dinner Party. You're terribly excited—you've been planning it for weeks, and you can't wait to use Your Good China and show off the way you've Redecorated Your Flat! However, it's Thursday, the Postman has just come and gone, and you've only heard from two of Your Guests. One, Polite Polly, telephoned the day she received the invitation and said that she would be delighted to come; is there anything she could bring? The second, Vague Victor, left a message saying that maybe he'd be there. Everyone else, it seems, is AWOL. You are ready to smack each of them Over the Head with a Canapé Tray! Why, in God's Name, do people not understand that R.S.V.P.-ing is Not Optional!

Oh, Dear Reader, the Etiquette Grrls feel for you. Not that any-one would dream of refusing an invitation to One of Our Parties, naturally, unless they had a *VERY* good reason, which of course they would immediately let us know about, but still, we understand your situation. How does one plan this dinner, when ten people May or May Not show up? How can you Set the Table Properly, decide Who Will Sit Where, or Shop for Food? How the hell are you supposed to know how much Artichoke Dip to make?? It is Simply Infuriating.

The EGs think the best tactic is to Take Matters into Your Own Hands. Call up the AWOL Guests, and ask if they've received the invitation you sent them. (There is always the Legitimate Possibility that someone's invitation is making a lengthy trip across your town, via, say, French Guiana, but Your Recalcitrant Friend may choose to tell you a Little White Lie at this point.) If they say they have not received it, give the invitation verbally and say that you hope they will be able to come—you were just concerned because you hadn't heard from them, so you thought something like that may have happened, since they usually R.S.V.P. *ever* so promptly. They will tell you whether or not they plan to attend, and that's that.

If, however, someone persists in Being Vague, we would recommend Being Firm. "I'm sorry, but you know how it is planning a Dinner Party—the number of people coming really makes a difference in how I prepare. I don't like to put you On the Spot, but could you please check your calendar and let me know sometime this afternoon if you'll be able to join us Saturday Evening? If I don't hear from you, I'll just assume we'll have to try for Another Time."

Also, you may have Guests who Say They Will Attend and then Cancel, or, worse, simply Do Not Show Up. Unless these people call you with a *Very* Good Excuse (e.g., hospitalization—not "Sorry, but *The Breakfast Club* was on TNT and I kind of got into watching it, so I just stayed home") and apologize, the EGs wouldn't invite them to Anything Else, Ever Again.

HOW TO APOLOGIZE

Sooner or Later, Dear Reader, everyone must Give an Apology. Even if you are the Most Polite and Conscientious Person Ever, something like the Weather, a Power Failure, or U.S. Air, will cause you to Inconvenience Someone Else, or to Back Out of an Invitation You've Accepted, etc. Then, Dear Reader, you must apologize. Here is how to accomplish this Gracefully.

First, what you say In Apology must actually *contain* An Apology. "I'm so sorry that I missed dinner. I know you were expecting me at seven, and I feel terrible to be so late." If you have an excuse, now is the time to offer it. "The subway car I was on broke down in a tunnel. We were there for two hours, and since we were

Underground, my Cell 'Phone didn't work." If you don't have an excuse, for heaven's sake, don't Make Up An Implausible One: "You'll never believe what happened—I gave someone a Thoracotomy with a Ballpoint Pen on the Subway, and he's fine now!" coming from someone who has No Medical Training and typically Faints at the Sight of Blood just adds Insult to Injury. Instead, tell the truth: "I lost track of time at the office. It won't happen again." If you feel it is warranted, offer to make it up to the person you're apologizing to: "Tomorrow night, let me cook dinner for you. I'd really like to show you how sorry I am." Do not, however, try to Buy Someone Off with Expensive Trinkets, particularly if you find yourself Screwing Up Often—this is Quite Insulting. Your Girlfriend does not want Yet Another Bracelet, she wants to know you take it seriously when you Make a Date with Her. Get Your Damn Act Together, and you won't need to Apologize So Much!

It's always More Mature to Apologize In Person, but if that is Truly Impossible—say you've offended someone So Terribly that they will not see you—you could try sending a Letter of Apology. In this, be formal, sincere, and contrite. "Dear Helen, I am so sorry I accused your dog of Eating My Prize Tomatoes. I said the most terrible things to you, and I'm quite ashamed of myself. This morning I spotted squirrels running off with several tomatoes, and I realized that your dog is in no way responsible. I hope you'll forgive me; I value our friendship, and I miss our conversations across the fence. If you can accept this apology—and I truly hope you will—would you come for coffee some evening? I'd like to tell you in person how sorry I am. Sincerely yours, Katherine." Notice there is no need to repeat the terrible things you said. "I am so sorry for calling you a Hideously Ugly, Thick-Headed Broad who has a Pathetic, Mange-Ridden, *STUPID* Dog that I've Always Despised," will not accomplish anything except remind Helen of Exactly How Much of a Jerk Katherine was. It also goes without saying that a Letter of Apology should be written on Your Best Writing Paper, and that you should compose it with Great Care.

LITTLE WHITE LIES

Some people flip out at the idea of Any Lie at All. We find that typically, these are Very Rude People who have Unrealistic World Views. Without the Little White Lie, Dear Reader, Polite Society would crumble. If you want to have Good Manners and Not Insult People, you will need to master this Important Bit of Rhetoric.

Note that the EGs are not talking about Inventing Vast, Complicated Lies, or Basing Your Life Around Them. Obviously, it is Not Good to invent a Fictitious Boy- or Girlfriend, or to tell new acquaintances you have a Very Important, High-Ranking Job when in fact you're Unemployed, etc. This kind of lie *ALWAYS* is discovered in a Most Embarrassing Way, and you will look Pathetic.

However, there is a Big Difference between saying, "I'm sorry, I can't go out with you because my boyfriend, Bono, the Irish Rock Star, would be Rather Upset By That," and saying, "I'm sorry, I just don't have time for a relationship right now." You might Very Well Have Time, for the Right Person, but there's no need to hurt the feelings of the Poor Boy asking you for a Date. Similarly, in the EGs' Opinion, it is always okay to have "already made plans" when you're invited to an event you really don't wish to attend (and aren't required to attend for the sake of propriety—you can't use a Little White Lie to get out of attending a Relative's Funeral, for example, but it would be okay to fib a bit to avoid a Dreary Dinner Party). The Less Embellishment you give a Little White Lie, the better. The EGs merely ask that if you ever Occasionally Fib, you do not attempt to catch your friends when they deal you a Little White Lie every once in a while, and that, in fact, you attempt to Learn Something from this. If Brenda is always busy every time you suggest the two of you Play Racquetball, perhaps she really doesn't fancy Playing Racquetball and is trying to be Nice About It. If you'd like to spend time with her, don't Probe for Details about what she'll be doing instead of Playing Racquetball With You, but suggest meeting for lunch sometime instead. See? It all Works Out, Dear Reader.

Your Small Pet

The Etiquette Grrls love Animals, Dear Reader, and you should, too! Pets are a smashing lot of fun, and there is nothing like a Small Furry Friend to make a Lonely Flat more enjoyable. However, we caution you: With the exception of Pet Rocks, pets are living, breathing creatures, and should be treated with Kindness and Respect. Also, much like Small Children, pets should learn to Behave Properly at All Times. We hope that our advice helps you to impart Beautiful Manners to Your Small Pet, and (even more importantly) to be a Kind, Responsible, Polite Pet Owner.

WHICH PET?

Obviously, your choice of a Small Pet will be determined by What Kinds of Animals You Particularly Like. So the EGs are not about to make rules like "Absolutely *no one* should have one of those Rat-like Miniature Pinschers," because, who knows, you may walk into your local SPCA and spot a Miniature Pinscher, rat-like though it is, that simply Melts Your Heart. However, whether you are considering adopting a cat or a dog, a ferret or a snake, or even a Prickly Little Hedgehog, you should keep a few important considerations in mind:

- It is THOR to acquire a Small Pet impulsively, particularly if you've given no thought to how much care it requires or, say, whether you're even allowed to *have* a kitten in Your Flat. If you are, for example, a Terribly Busy Investment Banker who frequently Jets Off to London for weeks on end, this might not be the Optimal Time for you to get two adorable Frisky Chocolate Lab Puppies. If you lack a yard and Aren't Much for Taking Long Walks, maybe a dog isn't the best choice for you at all. The Etiquette Grrls have seen too many Small Pets neglected or, worse, abandoned because Their Idiotic Owners did not think about these things, and such behavior makes us Very, Very Angry!

- It is also THOR to acquire a Small Pet if one has no idea how to care for it, no intention of training it, and no genuine regard for its Long-Term Well-Being. Remember, the adorable puppies will grow up, and they're yours for Quite a Few Years. If you don't want this responsibility, you shouldn't get them in the First Place. The EGs would like to smack people who think it's okay to Leave the Dog or Cat Outside All the Time, no matter the weather, or to let them run free near Busy Roads! Newsflash, everyone: Pets are Not Disposable!

- Does the Type of Pet you want suit Your Personality? Remember, Dear Reader, that Your Small Pet is an Extension of You. If you have a giant aquarium of Bloodthirsty Fighting Fish, that conveys a much different impression than owning a Fluffy Persian Kitten Named Priscilla. Do you want to be known as "That Girl Who Owns the Pit Bull" or "That Boy Who Walks the Hairless Cat"?

THE VERY STYLISH PET

The Stylish Pet is Graceful, yet Quirky. It is Beautifully Groomed. It is comfortable in most any environment, and with Most People. It is, of course, Highly Intelligent. Basically, you should aim to allow Your Pet's Personality to develop into one that, if it belonged to a Person, would make you want to invite that Person to a Cocktail Party. Your Pet should learn to Be Sociable! One of the EGs' Dear Friends is the owner of Gert, the Most Adorable, Sweet, Lovely Cat that we have ever met, and we are sure this is because Gert has been around Good Conversation, listened to Good Music, and had lots of opportunities to Socialize with Interesting People. Either that, or Our Dear Friend puts some sort of Happy-Smart-Nice Pills in Gert's food, but we highly, highly doubt that.

There are also All Manner of Adorable Pet Accessories one can buy! The EGs have found Darling Leather Collars at Coach, and, though this might be Un Peu Excessive, Tiffany's makes Engravable

Name Tags! On a more modest scale, there are lovely toys, comfy beds, and gourmet treats available for all species of pets—seek them out, and your Wee Beastie will surely appreciate it.

Finally, your Very Stylish Pet deserves a Very Stylish Name! The EGs think it is always smart to draw on Your Knowledge of Great Literature to find an appropriate name for your pet. Why have Mittens or Fluffy when you could have Oscar, or Eliot, or Esmé, or Austen? (One note: If there is a chance you'd like, one day, to use a particular name for One of Your Children, please do not give it to Your Small Pet. It would be most disconcerting for Your Daughter to share her name avec the Family Dog.)

THE WELL-BEHAVED PET

Most Pets make noise upon occasion. However, the Well-Behaved Pet does not make noise excessively, and will stop barking or howling or what have you Upon Command. We all want the Family Dog to bark loudly when a Prowler is Snooping About, but there is almost nothing more irritating than living next door to a Dog That Never Stops Barking, Dear Reader! Or a bird with a vocabulary of four words, two of which are Not Printable, who chatters to himself for Hours on End while one is trying to sleep on the other side of the Very Thin Apartment Wall! The Etiquette Grrls, and, for that matter, Everyone Else on This Planet, do not wish to have to Wear Earplugs to muffle the screeching cries of, "BIRDIE! BIRDIE! *&#*! HELLO? *#&#(! BIRDIE!" So please, Dear Reader, unless you live in the Middle of Nowhere, or in a Vacuum, where Sound Doesn't Carry, teach your pets to Be Quiet.

The Well-Behaved Pet is as Fastidious about His or Her Bathroom Habits as a Human Being should be. If for whatever reason (Illness, Advanced Age, Puppyhood, etc.) an otherwise Well-Behaved Pet has an Accident, then its owner must Clean It Up Immediately. That is all the EGs have to say upon this rather icky subject.

The Well-Behaved Pet is not Dangerous. Nor is it Aggressive.

A Small Child should be able to walk up to Your Cat/Dog/Bunny/
Chinchilla and not have the animal lunge at him. Purposeful Biting,
Scratching, etc., are not to be tolerated. Get thee to Obedience
School, stat!

The Well-Behaved Pet does not destroy things, particularly Expensive, Antique Furniture and Pretty Shoes. This is why Chew
Toys exist.

The Well-Behaved Pet does not attempt to steal food or beg.
Of course, it would be very cruel to put a Thanksgiving Turkey
out on a Low Table when you haven't fed Your Dog All Day, and
expect him to leave it be, but you know what we mean. You should
be able to pass Hors d'Oeuvres without the dog jumping up and
pawing at the tray, and if you host a Dinner Party, your guests
should be able to eat sans having the cat begging to partake of the
Fish Course.

Finally, the Well-Behaved Pet is happy when there are Visitors,
even when they are Total Strangers. However, the Well-Behaved
Pet does not get Hyper as All Hell whenever someone new walks
in—it is happy to be played with but not insistent upon it if the
newly-arrived guest prefers *not* to play Tug-of-War with the
Sopping-Wet Chew Toy.

HOW TO BEHAVE CORRECTLY AROUND SOMEONE ELSE'S PET
(PARTICULARLY IF YOU DON'T LIKE IT)

Oh, dear. You've arrived at your new friend Hortense's house and
there, running around the Living Room, is a *dog*. One of those
small, yippy ones that Scare the Bejesus Out of You. And it's Coming Right For You. Whatever do you do? Run out the front door,
screaming? Menacingly swing your handbag at it? Dive into the
Powder Room and refuse to leave? Dear Reader, all of the aforementioned options are Bad Choices.

The EGs understand that no one is *required* to like animals. We
just can't understand why some people don't. However, even if
you have a Profound Hatred of, say, birds, you must bear in mind

that if you are visiting someone who owns one, they probably love Their Canary, and you must make Every Effort to Maintain Your Composure. You are not allowed to make comments like, "Ugh. Cats are such Dirty, Sneaky Creatures," or, "The only Good Guinea Pig is a Dead Guinea Pig." You do not need to Fake Affection for the animal, but you shouldn't be Mean. Also, if the animal approaches you, simply ask its Owner if he'd mind calling it back. "I'm sorry, I am terribly allergic," is a convenient Little White Lie that can Work Wonders. You might also be honest: "Hortense, I'm terribly sorry, but I had no idea you had a Pug. One of them Mauled Me quite badly when I was a child, and I've tried for years to get over it, but I'm just terrified. Please excuse my shaking."

On the other hand, even if you Truly Love Animals, you may still exhibit Rude Behavior around someone else's pet. We should not even have to tell you this, but if the pet is Well-Behaved, do not encourage it to be Bad! If the dog is Not Allowed on the Couch (or if you do not know if the dog is Allowed on the Couch), do not pat the cushion next to you and say, "C'mon up, Trixie!" Don't, especially, take it upon yourself to feed someone else's pet Food It Is Not Supposed to Have. If you give the kitten a bite of your Salmon Canapé, she just might refuse, from that moment on, to consume Dry Kitten Food ever again. Trust the EGs, this will not please her Owners, who, unless they are Microsoft Executives or something, are not likely to have the Financial Wherewithal to supply Mittens with a Steady Diet of Smoked Salmon.

What to do if Someone Else's Pet is just Ill-Behaved, Obnoxious, Foul-Smelling, or Irritating? Attempt, as best you can, to Hold Your Tongue. If the dog keeps jumping up in your lap, you may say, "Cujo, *DOWN!*" in a Firm Voice, or even ask its owners if there's something particular you should say or do to get Cujo to Cease and Desist. If the Owners do not Help You Out, or, worse, think it's funny to have Their Maniacal Mutt bothering you, then the EGs would suggest you socialize with them only in locations where Darling Cujo cannot be present.

HOW TO BE A POLITE PET OWNER

This brings us, Dear Reader, to another Important Point. As a Pet Owner, you absolutely must keep an eye on how your guests react to your pets! If a guest seems even *slightly* upset, then be the Bigger Person and let Cujo play in the backyard for a bit. If someone is Sneezing Violently, you might ask if it'd help if you put the cats in the bedroom for a while, or if perhaps she'd be more comfortable if you had coffee at the Café Down the Street. Also, please remember, things which you may consider to be Your Pet's Adorable Foibles may disgust, anger, or just annoy Everyone Else. If you observe any reactions like this from your guests, we suggest you remove the pet to another part of the house and consider if it really *is* all that adorable for the cat to attempt to Nurse on an Unsuspecting Stranger's Cashmere Sweater. If you come to the conclusion that It Is Not (and, Dear Reader, trust us, It Is *Not*), then take steps to modify Kitty's behavior.

One last thing: While your pet may seem Practically Human, the Etiquette Grrls beg to remind you that Your Guests have come to see *you*, not to Spend Time With Your Pet. If your small pet is there, Minding His Own Beeswax, that is all well and good; as is it fine for him to come over to say hello and play for a bit with a guest who Shows an Interest in him. However, your guests probably do not want to see Fido's Repertoire of Tricks again if they've seen them the last time they visited. They also probably do not fancy a trip into the yard to see Fido fetch sticks if they're wearing High Heels.

Lesley Carlin is a New Englander—in terms of both Her Birthplace and Her Temperament. After seven years of Catholic School, which she fondly compares to Chinese Water Torture, she enrolled at a small Massachusetts prep school, whence she graduated as a member of the last all-girls class. Lesley continued her studies at Princeton, where she majored in English Literature and Creative Writing and learned how to Mix a Mean G&T. She picked up her A.B. in 1995, packed up the Etiquette Volvo, and moved to Ann Arbor, Michigan, to begin Graduate Work in Creative Writing, courtesy of a Jacob Javits Fellowship. After earning her M.F.A. in 1997, Lesley embarked upon what is obviously a natural career path for a Trained Poet; she is now the Managing Editor and Site Producer for an Internet Start-Up. Lesley lives outside Boston.

Honore McDonough Ervin, who was raised in Washington, D.C., London, and Massachusetts, attended the all-girls Westover School, but transferred in order to be one of the first girls to graduate from Portsmouth Abbey School in Rhode Island, where she tried her damnedest to instruct her nearly all-male classmates in The Art of Gracious Living. She then settled at Chatham College in Pittsburgh, Pennsylvania, where she majored in Art History and English, graduating in 1997. While pursuing graduate studies at the University of Virginia, she discovered that contrary to popular belief, and much to her Bitter Disappointment, that Southern Living does not, in fact, entail quaint activities such as sipping Mint Juleps on the veranda and singing songs about the Swanee River. Honore currently resides in Massachusetts, but can frequently be found at The Algonquin Hotel in New York City, Tossing Back a Gin Gimlet (up, please!), or a G&T (Thank you, and charge it, please!), and playing the Resident Wit.

The Etiquette Grrls enjoy traveling (first class, whenever possible), drinking stiff G&Ts (with Bombay Sapphire, please), and shopping for vintage clothing. "Accomplished" young women in the Jane Austen sense of the word, they were taught at very young ages how to play the piano, dance divinely, eat artichokes properly, and spot Good Jewelry. They are vicious badminton players! You will find the Etiquette Grrls listening to Cake, road-tripping to exclusive oceanfront towns, and collecting Lilly Pulitzer dresses. The Etiquette Grrls throw Fabulous Parties, renowned all over the Eastern Seaboard, from the classic A Very Boozy Thanksgiving to impromptu soirées for which even poor, starving graduate students wear their smartest cocktail attire. A frequent response from first-time guests at the Etiquette Grrls' parties is, "I had no idea a party without a keg and tequila shots could be so much fun!" In the Etiquette Volvo, which has over 100,000 miles on it, they travel the world, fighting rudeness with cutting remarks, hilarious observations, and, always, elegance and grace.

The Etiquette Grrls are not to be trifled with.